TOE BY TOE®

A Highly Structured Multi-Sensory Phonetic Approach to Literacy

Keda Cowling Cert Ed & Harry Cowling B.A.Hons

Published in 1993 by
K & H Cowling
Baildon, West Yorkshire

ISBN O 9522564 0 1

To Peter, my first dyslexic pupil, with regret that my work in 1970 was not sufficiently developed for you to reap those benefits which *Toe by Toe* has since bestowed on countless others. *Toe by Toe*'s success was born from your frustration.

With love K.C.

A little giant made of steel sleeps by the river. H.C.

Acknowledgements

Toe by Toe has been developed over a period of twenty-five years. The creator of the system - **Keda Cowling** - was forced to adopt a single-minded and sometimes ruthless approach to her own work. Every aspect of *Toe by Toe* has been subjected to vigorous testing and verification.

The early development of *Toe by Toe* was largely undertaken without assistance and often in the face of professional hostility. Over the last five years her family awoke to the idea that Keda Cowling was not in the last throes of madness and began to give her the assistance she so badly needed.
This book owes little to orthodox theories and methods of Special Needs teaching. However, it does acknowledge the support of those children, parents and enlightened teachers whose faith in her methods have gained her the highest regard and gained them an unprecedented level of success. H.C.

Kelsey Cowling's diligent testing of every exercise in this book and constant involvement with all aspects of Toe by Toe's development have been invaluable. He has proved by his dedication and patience to be a fine tutor, advisor and - sometimes - referee.

Dr. David Briggs BSc. (Hons) MSc. (Psychopathology) A.B.PsS, Dip. Psych, Ph.d. Chartered Psychologist, Consultant to the Dyslexia Institute. In the embryonic years David Briggs had enough faith in my methods to introduce and recommend me to so many dyslexic students. I will always be grateful for his support and encouragement. **K.C.**

I would like to thank **Stan Hinchcliffe** for his encouragement. My son and I are grateful for his services as a proof-reader. **K.C**.

Albert Cowling is a quiet, gentle, cheerful man who prefers the background to the spotlight. He is a wonderful father and a patient husband. The publication of this manual has involved turning the home he built into a workshop, school, office, telephone exchange and boxing-ring. He never uttered one word of complaint. Thanks Dad!

Who will benefit from this book?

Any child with reading difficulties especially those who have been diagnosed as having specific learning difficulties (dyslexia).

Adults who have weak reading skills.

Parents who have weak reading skills and would like to learn alongside their children.

Special needs teachers.

Support assistants working with statemented children under the direction of class teachers.

Any classroom assistant helping a child with reading difficulties.

The authors believe that at least twenty per cent of the population need this book.

Photo-copying

Teachers often ask us whether *Toe by Toe* is suitable for photo-copying. *Toe by Toe* has been 25 years in development: a painstaking process of trial and error, using different structures, countless control groups and endless teaching of children and adults with the severest difficulties. The end product is so finely structured that we decided to call it *Toe by Toe*. To describe it as a '**step by step**' system would not describe the integrated, comprehensive and finely structured system which lies within these pages.

Photo-copying would lead to a piecemeal arrangement whereby the instructions and exercises would become separated and the vital diagnostic elements of Toe by Toe would be overturned in order that schools could save what would amount to very little. The ultimate cost would be borne by frustrated students whose progress would be limited.

When we say that every child should have her/his own book we speak from experience. The text is a record of each child's personal achievement. It is a history of their struggle to read and become part of an environment from which they have been alienated. It is also very inexpensive.

For the above reasons we are not members of the Copyright Licensing Agency. We will do our utmost to ensure that photocopying of this text does not take place.

You must complete every exercise in this book.
You must start from the first exercise.

Before You Start!

Generally, the format of the text is divided into three areas: **Other information, Instructions** and **Exercises.**

Other information: The information in this section is for those people who are interested in, or may question, the methodology which supports *Toe by Toe*. Where necessary, it will give more details of the exercises and why they have been included.

Instructions: These are set out as coaching boxes and are headed: **Coach**

Exercises: It is vital when using *Toe by Toe* that progress is carefully recorded. *Toe by Toe* progresses by minute steps with different skills introduced in a calculated order. The grid makes sure that coaches and their students do not omit any of the skills essential for progress through later exercises.

Do not start in the middle of the book. If you are under the impression that your student is too advanced for the early exercises and attempt to take short cuts, you will undermine both the structure of the book and, inevitably, the confidence of your student. If your student has the ability to move quickly through the exercises, you will not have to wait long before you reach his/her level.

Toe by Toe has been created so that anyone with a moderate reading ability will be able to teach others to read. *Toe by Toe* recognises that reading problems are often inherited and that some parents will struggle to adapt to a system which is too complex. If you belong to this group of people and wish to coach your child without reading the introductory pages, you may turn to the first 'coaching box' on **page 8** and begin. The coaching boxes contain all the information needed to coach your student. You do not have to read the **'Other information'** sections.

Some questions answered

Q: Is this an activity book for children to work with by themselves?
A: **No! Toe by Toe** requires that each child has a reading coach for every exercise; it teaches children to read and parents to teach.

Q: Why has **Toe by Toe** neglected to provide a teacher's book?
A: Teachers will be the first to admit that they do not have the time to be constantly checking a manual. Each **Toe by Toe** exercise is accompanied by its own coaching box.

Q: Is this book solely for the use of teachers or other professionals?
A: **No!** Teachers are often restricted by classroom procedures. Parents have no such procedures to inhibit them. They start with a 'clean slate'.

Q: Will **Toe by Toe** compromise the reading attainment targets in the National Curriculum?
A: **No! Toe by Toe** has proved in practice that, with the minimum of administrative commitment, it can accelerate the reading age of a student, with or without reading difficulties, far in advance of his/her chronological age.

Q: Why does a child need to have three consecutive ticks before a word can be considered learned?
A: Students with reading difficulties, particularly dyslexics, will establish a word in their short-term memory but they are likely to forget it just as easily unless we bond the word in their long-term memory.

Q: Why is **Toe by Toe** so pedantic?

A: This is a most welcome complaint. **Toe by Toe** has proved in practice that children or adults who have learning difficulties make very slow progress if they are taught by less structured methods. Reading coaches using **Toe by Toe** know at a glance the weaknesses of their students and can rectify them. One cannot be confident that any element of an exercise has been learned unless we can provide positive evidence on three consecutive occasions.

Q: Why doesn't the manual contain a list of contents?

A: **Toe by Toe** is a finely structured programme. A list of contents might tempt some coaches to begin coaching part way through the text. We must ensure that the programme is followed as it is presented.

Q: Would it not have been easier to use the International Phonetic Alphabet to describe the basic sounds in the relevant exercises?

A: The International Phonetic Alphabet is a useful method for learning the pronunciation of foreign words or learning how to pronounce unfamiliar words in a dictionary. However, before one uses a dictionary one must first of all be able to read and spell. The I.P.A. does not account for regional variations. In order to overcome this problem **Toe by Toe** uses examples of words containing a particular skill.

Q: Will **Toe by Toe** help children who prefer to learn by playing games etc.?

A: The question implies that education is not enjoyable. **Toe by Toe** gives children success and success is a far more powerful and enjoyable spur to education than any game. The question also implies that students with reading difficulties are only capable of learning through entertainment. Most people with reading difficulties find this view patronising. **Toe by Toe** considers all learners to be educable equals.

About Toe by Toe

The **Toe by Toe** multi-sensory teaching method has been developed over twenty-five years. It arose out of the needs of a teacher whose abundant dedication and patience were still not enough to teach all of her students to be competent readers. Out of the struggle to meet the needs of these children came the recognition of the role played by dyslexia. Consequent upon that recognition came the painstaking development of a system for the teaching of reading which the authors believe to be unsurpassed in its record of success.

Toe by Toe is the ultimate tool for the teaching of reading. It is methodical, gradual, finely structured, measurable, easy to use and, above all, highly successful.

Toe by Toe does not deal in hyperbole. Its success has been witnessed, recorded, lauded by many and coveted by others. If **Toe by Toe** were to be adopted nationally it would overturn current trends in special needs teaching. It is both cheap and effective. It is easy to use and progress can be measured throughout the book. The name '**Toe by Toe**' describes a structure too finely graded to be described as 'step by step'. It is ideal for dyslexics and other students with reading difficulties.

Toe by Toe's syllable division will have its critics. Conventional syllable division places an emphasis on syllable stress. The syllable division used in **Toe by Toe** deals with word building alone. **Toe by Toe** asks: "Did you learn to read polysyllabic words correctly as a result of learning correct stress patterns or did you learn stresses by listening to the sound of words?" **Toe by Toe** teaches children to read polysyllabic words through syllable division. Students will learn the stresses like anyone else; through hearing the patterns of speech in general usage. We need children to read polysyllabic words quickly.

Certain conventions of grammar have been abandoned in the early stages of the book. This is essentially a word building manual and in the early exercises we are limited to the most simple phonic words. The sentences will often sound stilted and awkward. Our early sentences are bound by the skills we have taught. For example: in the first few exercises there are no words containing vowel combinations. As more skills are acquired, the sentences will become more flexible and less stilted.

Many of **Toe by Toe**'s sentences are deliberately contrived in order that a student will build a word rather than guess it from the context. However, as it would be impossible to construct our sentences without the use of some non-phonic words, we have included a number of them (we have called them **Link Words**) in order that we can make steady progress through the text.

In the later exercises your student will be introduced to words which are unlikely to form part of his/her vocabulary. These words, when read correctly, will provide evidence of the effectiveness of the **Toe by Toe** word building method.

Harry Cowling

How and why it works

After many years of research and constant trial, Keda Cowling arrived at a highly structured and very successful working system. It combines a multi-sensory approach with a memory bonding technique.

It is vital to **Toe by Toe** that a barely formed image of a word which is beginning to slip from a student's memory is grasped at that point and forged by the struggle to recall it. Words taught in this way have a greater chance of staying in the student's long-term memory and it is of paramount importance that the exercises are carried out in a timed and structured manner.

Students have their own book which is all the equipment necessary for coaching to begin. Coaching can be undertaken with the minimum of preparation; the book in front of the student and a pen for the coach. Success is visible and success is all the encouragement a student needs.

The **Toe by Toe** grid system allows a student to be coached both at home and in school by different coaches. At a glance, a coach can find the exact point where a student left an exercise.

A note on spelling

Most people learn to spell by a constant process of recollection of the printed word. Generally, they learn by reading. Thus, spelling and reading becomes a mutual activity. People with reading difficulties are disadvantaged in that, not only are they disinclined to pick up a book and read, they are also less likely to indulge in other activities such as 'Monopoly' or 'Scrabble' which would otherwise enhance their reading skills. Furthermore, their image recall is so weak that, even if they attain a good reading level, their spelling will not improve *pro rata.*

Students with reading difficulties tend to spell phonetically, they spell a word as it sounds. 'Enough' will often be spelt 'inuff' and 'said' will be spelt 'sed'. These students can be taught to read far more easily than they can be taught to spell for the above mentioned reasons.

Fundamental to any spelling programme is the ability to read fluently and **Toe by Toe** is designed to achieve an unprecedented level of fluency in people who would not otherwise be able to read words of more than two syllables. The multi-sensory **Say it & Write it** pages will assist the student in the spelling of many words. However, the book is essentially a programme for the teaching of reading.

In the majority of our word building exercises we need to know that a student can read a word correctly on three separate occasions. If a student does not know a word or reads a word incorrectly, we place a dot in the appropriate box. Crosses are forbidden. People with learning difficulties are too familiar with crosses; they symbolise failure. A word read correctly earns a tick or a stroke.

The book is designed to promote daily progress as follows:

Day 1
1. Place the date in the boxes at the top of the grid. Our example starts on the fifth of September.
2. Ask the student to read the letter sounds or words in the column, ticking or dotting as you move down.
3. When you have completed one column, move to the next column and ask the student the letter sounds or words. Once more, tick or dot the letter sounds or words.
4. Continue as above for a period of no longer than 20 minutes.

Day 2 and Day 3
Go to the page on which you started Day 1.
Write the date next to the previous day's date.
Repeat checking the grid as for Day 1

Day 4 and after
Repeat as previous days except that you should omit words which have 3 ticks.

You may work on as many exercises as twenty minutes allow. If a word or sound has not gained three consecutive ticks by the end of an exercise (see **sh** in the last column of the example page) refer it to the next multi-sensory page (**page 26**). You will find multi-sensory pages at intervals throughout the text.

Here is an example of a completed grid.

Day	5	6	7	8	9
Month	9	9	9	9	9
u	/	/	/		
h	/	/	/		
c	/	/	/		
x	/	/	/		
e	/	/	/		
f	/	/	/		
g	/	/	/		
b	·	·	/	/	/
i	/	/	/		
j	/	/	/		
n	/	/	/		
l	/	·	/	/	/

Day	5	6	7	8	9
Month	9	9	9	9	9
m	/	/	/		
k	/	/	/		
o	/	/	/		
p	·	/	/	/	
qu	/	/	/		
r	/	/	/		
z	/	/	/		
t	/	/	/		
a	/	/	/		
v	/	/	/		
w	/	/	/		
d	·	·	/	/	/

Day	5	6	7	8	9
Month	9	9	9	9	9
y	/	/	/		
s	/	/	/		
sh	·	·	/	/	/
th	·	/	/	/	
ch	·	·	/	/	/
ck	·	/	/	/	
	/	/	/		
A	/	/	/		
W	/	/	/		
D	/	/	/		
E	/	/	/		
Z	/	·	/	/	/

Day	5	6	7	8	9
Month	9	9	9	9	9
G	/	/	/		
H	/	/	/		
I	/	/	/		
J	/	/	/		
M	/	/	/		
L	/	/	/		
K	/	/	/		
P	/	/	/		
O	/	/	/		
N	/	/	/		
T	/	/	/		
R	/	/	/		

Day	5	6	7	8	9
Month	9	9	9	9	9
S	/	/	/		
Qu	·	·	/	/	/
U	/	/	/		
V	/	/	/		
C	/	/	/		
X	/	/	/		
Y	/	/	/		
F	/	/	/		
B	/	/	/		
Th	/	·	/	/	/
Sh	·	·	·	/	/
Ch	/	/	/		

Remember:

1. Always begin the day's coaching by placing the date next to the date of the previous day's exercise.
2. Progress is much quicker if the exercises are undertaken on a daily basis but it doesn't matter if you skip the odd day.
3. These are basic instructions. Each exercise has its own individual coaching tips.

Other Information

Letter sounds

Letter names only serve to confuse early readers, particularly those with reading difficulties. We must insist that phonic sounds are used throughout the text. We have found on many occasions that students with severe reading problems have had their progress hampered by well meaning friends or parents who have taught them the names of the consonants in the alphabet.

Spelling too, can be seriously hampered. The word which always springs to mind is: **'help'**. This was spelt **'lp'** by one of our students and was a typical example of his spelling. He could not hear the short vowel sound of **'e'** because it was swamped by the sound of **'el'** which he translated into the name of the letter **'L'**.

The alphabet order is not necessary for the teaching of reading. It is at best a spelling tool used to find words in a dictionary. Unless it is a phonetic dictionary, people with reading difficulties will find that a pocket word finder is of far more use.

Coach

Let the student look at the pictures and letters.

Each picture is accompanied by the initial letter; both small and capital. We need the student to know the *sound* of the letter and not its name.

We need **a** for apple and **b** for ball. We do not want **ay bee see**

Make sure the student knows the letter sounds which accompany the pictures before moving to the next exercise.

Note: small and capital letters are also known as *lower* and *upper case*.

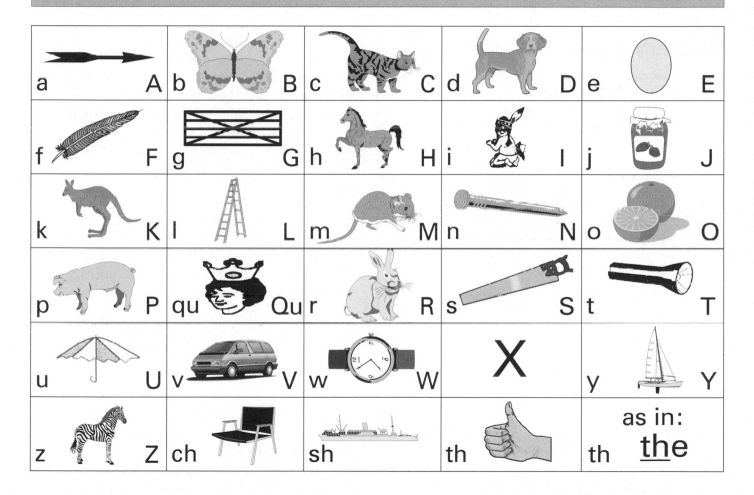

a A	b B	c C	d D	e E
f F	g G	h H	i I	j J
k K	l L	m M	n N	o O
p P	qu Qu	r R	s S	t T
u U	v V	w W	X	y Y
z Z	ch	sh	th	th as in: <u>the</u>

Other Information

Letter sounds continued

The sounds **sh**, **ch**, **th**, **ck** and **qu** will also be dealt with in depth in a later exercise.

The alphabet in this exercise has been rearranged to stop the student from 'chanting' the sounds. It is important that they recognise and say the letters and not just recall them by association with the sound of the preceding letter. Once more we require the letter sounds only.

Coach

Tick the positives (the sounds the student knows) and dot the negatives (the sounds the student doesn't know). Three ticks in a row (consecutive) are needed to complete the exercise. Each tick must be earned on a different day.

If you are unsure of the grid marking system, you may look at the example grid on **page 9**. Remember! We need the letter sounds only and not **ay**, **bee**, **see**…etc. This also applies to capital letters.

Make sure your student knows the letter sounds before moving to the next exercise. The letters **ck** make the single sound of the letter **c**.

If the student has difficulty with a particular letter, you may refer him/her to the pictures on the previous page.

Day	1	4			Day	2	4			Day	2	4			Day	2	4			Day	2	4		
Month	3	3			Month	3	3			Month	3	3			Month	3	3			Month	3	3		
u					m					y					G					S				
h					k					s					H					Qu				
c					o					sh					I					U				
x					p					th					J					V				
e					qu					ch					M					C				
f					r					ck					L					X				
g					z										K					Y				
b					t					A					P					F				
i					a					W					O					B				
j					v					D					N					Th				
n					w					E					T					Sh				
l					d					Z					R					Ch				

A black pen makes the dots stand out and makes the grid easier to check.

Coach

Make sure the student understands that these are not real words. They are syllables (chunks of words). The student must now say the letter sounds; **un** as in **un**der, **ab** as in **ab**stract. Show how the letter sounds slide together to form the sound of the syllable. Give the short sound **e** then the sound **m** and then 'slide' them together to form **em**. Should you have difficulty with the three letter syllables, ask for the last two letters first.

Examples

fet: ask the student to say the last two letters; in this case **et** and then ask him/her to put the first letter **f** on the front and slide them together and say '**fet**'.

feb: remove the first letter and say the last two i.e. **eb** then put the first letter back and slide them together to say '**feb**'.

There are three pages to this exercise.

Three consecutive ticks are needed before we can consider a word to have been placed in the student's long-term memory.

Once started and dated, always complete the column. Do not start a column which you may not complete.

Day	4						
Month	7						
af							
ab							
ag							
ap							
ad							
av							
ix							
cam							
lab							
fab							
bam							

Day	4						
Month	3						
fam							
rep							
fep							
en							
ep							
ket							
ux							
seg							
ob							
os							
poth							

Day	4						
Month	3						
sith							
es							
ef							
coff							
sonn							
tath							
ex							
lop							
dess							
ol							
pidd							

Day	5										
Month	3										
uff											
pum											
supp											
nudd											
bex											
og											
riff											
tiff											
ub											
lom											
goff											

Day	5										
Month	3										
ris											
tepp											
lan											
cadd											
thax											
sott											
luss											
ag											
bon											
dap											
ock											

Day	5										
Month	3										
ack											
ig											
id											
diff											
dax											
pedd											
rell											
tem											
romm											
liff											
obb											

Day									
Month									
hib									
piff									
idd									
uf									
bonn									
taf									
igg									
hap									
tesh									
lib									
todd									

Day									
Month									
honn									
osh									
uch									
libb									
agg									
hef									
ogg									
ish									
pesh									
temm									
hiff									

Day									
Month									
hep									
abb									
hoff									
hon									
tox									
gax									
cham									
happ									
peth									
osh									
hubb									

Other Information

Real Words

It may seem odd that nonsense words should come before real words. However, every exercise in this book has been planned.

Nonsense words are designed to stop the student from pre-empting the answer through association. We are aware that the sound of the word **vet** will be established more quickly than **tev** but we are not interested in **Look and Say** techniques at this stage. We are anxious that students should be building words from the letters before them.

Real satisfaction will be gained when the student realizes that he or she can read real words easily.

Coach

Point out that this exercise is the same as the previous exercise but this time the words are real. They are words of one syllable. They are *one chunk* words. Please follow the grid system and don't feel that your student can miss any part of any exercise.

These are simple words but if you neglect them or choose to ignore the minimum twenty-four hour gap between attempts the result will be frustration. The usual three ticks are needed.

Link Words

Link words must be taught by **Look and Say**. Before you start work on a column, ask your student to read the word in the shaded area at the bottom. If s/he knows the word place a tick in the box. If not, tell your student the word, make him/her repeat it; place a dot in the box.

When you reach the bottom of the column, ask your student to read any negative **Link Words** again. Ask your student to read the negative **Link Words** once more at the end of each session. **Remember!** Negatives do not receive ticks on the day they are coached. Repeat the exercise after a period of twenty-four hours; not before!

Day											Day											Day										
Month											Month											Month										
it											is											far										
as											pan											if										
an											ran											can										
am											sip											pin										
pot											let											win										
hat											bun											cat										
nit											pet											sit										
rot											cot											nun										
gun											pit											set										
ram											bat											dot										
have											to											and										

Other Information

Three Letter Syllables with 's' at the end

We do not need to explain the difference between a plural and a change in tense. It is enough to say that **'s'** at the end of a word can mean more than one.

Coach

Explain to your student that the letter **S** at the end of a word can mean more than one.

If s/he seems to have difficulty, try the word without the **S**. When the word can be read easily without the **S**, you may then add it to the word and try once more.

Make sure your student knows that these are real words.

Each word needs to earn three consecutive ticks.

Each tick must be earned on a different day.

Tick the positives and dot the negatives.

Make sure you work on any negatives before you leave the page.

Day											Day											Day										
Month											Month											Month										
cot											red											sob										
cots											digs											tab										
fan											can											tins										
fans											bins											lit										
bat											not											fad										
bats											sags											sins										
pig											put											pegs										
pigs											cabs											pets										
jig											him											get										
jigs											fog											pans										
what											he											here										

Other Information

Grammar is limited by the words containing the skills the student has learned so far and many of our sentences have been made deliberately awkward which forces the student to look at the words and not the context. Statements will be treated as sentences. A plethora of inverted commas and semicolons can create panic. The classic response is: "How do I read these tadpoles?"

You can teach students the more complex principles of punctuation when they have mastered the mechanics of reading.

The 'e' is mute at the end of the word 'the' so we regard it as a non-phonic word but students with the severest reading difficulties can still read the word. Therefore, it will not be used as a **Link Word**.

As a new skill is introduced it will be used in the subsequent sentences.

Coach

Ask the student to read the sentences. If all the words are read correctly tick the box.

1. Underline any words in a sentence which have not been read correctly and coach them.

2. After a period of **not less** than twenty-four hours you must ask the student to attempt the underlined words once more. When the student knows the word put a bar **(/)** through the underline with a pencil.

3. Tick the box when all the underlined words in a sentence have been barred. Dates are not required. However, you must keep returning to the underlined words until all boxes have been ticked.

The full sentence needs to be read once only but the underlined words must then be coached.

Never bar a word on the day that you coach it.

He can put the big dog in here with the fat ram.

The pet cat is with the duck in the big pen.

Pass the bag with the jam and the bun to Mack and Tim.

What is that on the lid of the big box and can I have it?

The pig and the dog will have fun in the wet mud.

If he has a fox for a pet he will have to put the hen in the hut.

Tim is here with Tom and not with Pam, Meg or Sam.

Pick up the egg and put it in here and not in the pan.

Run to Dan and tell him that Jack is here and not in the den.

What has Mick put in the big red sack?

Ben and Kim have fun in the hot sun.

Put on a hat if it is wet and run to the top of the hill.

The big fat cat will have to sit on the rock and not on the mat.

He will sit on the sack and not on the rug.

He sat on the log and not on the big tin.

Bat before ball says 'b'.

The letters **b** and **d** can cause all manner of problems for people with reading difficulties. Remind your student that **bat before ball says b**.

The first two columns contain groups of letters. Working from left to right; ask your student to read each letter in a group. As soon as a mistake is made you must dot the grid and move immediately to the next group of letters. Treat the last column as an ordinary exercise.

Some students will struggle to get three consecutive ticks on this exercise. Dates

are not necessary. You may use this exercise as often as you like. The bat and

ball motif is very useful. Remind your student that the bat goes before the ball.

b d o p d p d b				b p b o d o p d				pob		
b p b o b o d d				d p o p d o b d				pab		
p o p o d b p d				b p o b o b p d				pud		
b o p p d p b p				p o d o b o d p				dub		
p b o d o b d b				b o d p o b o d				bod		
b o d p o b b d				p o p d b o d b				dob		
d p o p b o d b				d o p d b o b b				pid		
p d b b o d o p				d o b d o d p d				deb		

We still need the short sound of the letters.

Coach

On the opposite page you will see an example of a multi-sensory **'Say it Write it'** grid.

If previous pages have revealed any difficulties such as an inability to earn three consecutive ticks; use these grids for additional coaching as follows:-

1   The coach must print the words (real or nonsense) in the shaded boxes, saying the word at the same time.

2   The student must then do exactly the same, but continue all the way down as the example shows - **always saying the word as s/he writes it**.

The pattern of flow in **joined up** writing helps to stimulate the student's memory of a word shape. This is particularly useful in spelling polysyllabic words. However, **Toe by Toe** is essentially a reading method designed to accelerate a student's ability to read the printed word quickly and accurately.

Very young students may not have reached the **joined up** writing stage. Do not put pressure on them to do so.

e.g.	here	luss	osh	ath	rock	with
say it	here	luss	osh	ath	rock	with
say it	here	luss	osh	ath	rock	with
say it	here	luss	osh	ath	rock	with
say it	here	luss	osh	ath	rock	with
say it	here	luss	osh	ath	rock	with
say it	here	luss	osh	ath	rock	with
say it	here	luss	osh	ath	rock	with
say it	here	luss	osh	ath	rock	with
say it	here	luss	osh	ath	rock	with
say it	here	luss	osh	ath	rock	with
say it	here	luss	osh	ath	rock	with

Check any previously completed grids for words which have not earned three ticks in a row.

here	here	luss	osh	ath	rock	with
	here					

Coach

Identification of Initial Blends using Real Words

By initial blends we mean the combination of letters that introduce us to the word. These letters are consonants. We will discuss them later. Opposite are some examples. The blends are in the left hand column, the whole word in the right.

The blends and words in the two columns within the red square are for you to read alone. **The student must not attempt to read them.**

Read both columns out loud; blend followed by word. i.e. **fl** then **flag** until the student becomes aware of what is meant by a blend. When this has been established, you may repeat the word to the student and ask for the blend. When you have completed the list you may try the exercise on the opposite page.

The fourth column in the exercise on the opposite page contains a repetition of certain blends which often cause confusion.

fl	flag	thr	thrush
gr	grass	pl	plant
sw	swing	st	stick
br	bridge	pr	prince
cr	crisps	dr	drum
fr	frog	tr	train
bl	blue	cl	cloud
gl	glue	sm	smile
qu	queen	dw	dwarf
sn	snail	spl	splash
tw	twig	scr	screw
sk	sky	str	string
sl	slipper	spr	spring
sp	spoon	squ	squid

Day									
Month									
sn									
pl									
sl									
st									
fr									
gl									
sp									
sl									
tr									
st									
cr									
sw									
br									

Day									
Month									
cl									
sk									
bl									
sp									
gr									
dr									
tw									
dw									
sl									
fl									
st									
sm									
qu									

Day									
Month									
str									
spr									
scr									
spl									
shr									
thr									
squ									
spl									
shr									
scr									
thr									
spl									
shr									

Day									
Month									
bl									
dr									
pl									
pr									
gr									
gl									
fl									
fr									
bl									
gr									
fl									
cl									
pr									

Other Information

Nonsense Words

The format for the majority of Toe by Toe's exercises begins with nonsense words which involve the skill we wish to introduce.

Once a student is familiar with the skills used in nonsense words, we can be confident that real words will not cause problems.

Coach

Make sure your student knows that these are nonsense words.

Each word needs to earn three consecutive ticks.

Each tick must be earned on a different day.

Tick the positives and dot the negatives.

Make sure you work on any negatives before you leave the page.

Day						Day						Day						Day					
Month						Month						Month						Month					
flim						blit						slif						tribb					
flen						blat						slof						trobb					
grif						glif						spig						clim					
gref						gled						spog						clom					
swip						quon						plin						smett					
swep						quep						plon						smitt					
brid						snig						stib						shrell					
brod						sneg						stob						scrim					
crip						twip						prin						thrip					
crup						twop						pran						splon					
frim						skup						drig						scriff					
frem						skap						drog						sprib					

Other Information

Real Words

Coach

Make sure your student knows that these are real words.

Each word needs to earn three consecutive ticks.

Each tick must be earned on a different day.

Tick the positives and dot the negatives.

Make sure you work on any negatives before you leave the page.

Remember! The Link Words in the shaded boxes must be taught by **Look & Say** methods.

This exercise is three pages long.

Day								Day								Day								Day							
Month								**Month**								**Month**								**Month**							
slab								span								tram								brat							
slat								spin								trim								bred							
slop								spot								trot								stab							
slum								spit								trap								stop							
slap								spun								trod								stem							
sled								spat								tress								staff							
slid								spud								trip								step							
slot								sprig								truss								still							
slit								sprat								brag								stag							
slog								slub								brim								drip							
slam								slip								bran								drop							
slim								slug								brass								drag							
was								**so**								**come**								**why**							

Day								Day								Day								Day							
Month								Month								Month								Month							
stun								skin								clod								drill							
stiff								swag								clot								drug							
plan								swam								club								glad							
plot								swell								clog								glut							
plus								swill								clad								gloss							
plug								swim								class								glib							
plod								crab								clip								glass							
skiff								crag								clam								glum							
skid								cram								clap								glen							
skill								crop								dram								smug							
skull								cross								drum								smog							
skip								crib								drab								smut							
you								we								who								does							

Day							Day							Day							Day						
Month							Month							Month							Month						
prop							fluff							snuff							grog						
prom							floss							snub							grit						
pram							flit							twig							grim						
press							fret							twill							grin						
prod							from							twin							grip						
prim							frill							grab							blot						
flap							Fred							gruff							bluff						
flax							frizz							grub							bled						
flab							snag							Gran							bliss						
flan							snap							grid							blob						
flux							snip							grass							blab						
flag							snob							grill							bless						
girl							came							before							do						

Other Information

Real Words

Unlike the previous exercise, where words with the same initial blend were grouped together, the blends in this exercise have been mixed in order that the student learns to move quickly between different blends.

Coach

Make sure your student knows that these are real words.

Each word needs to earn three consecutive ticks.

Each tick must be earned on a different day.

Tick the positives and dot the negatives.

Make sure you work on any negatives before you leave the page.

Day							Day							Day							Day						
Month							Month							Month							Month						
brag							drag							prop							glen						
drab							flap							skip							skim						
trot							glib							spin							flan						
slob							grim							blot							twill						
spun							fled							spill							plus						
glad							pram							glass							snob						
clog							drop							bliss							flit						
slap							trod							scuff							glut						
slot							clip							flab							trip						
flex							crux							trim							brass						
fox							span							stem							crop						
slum							scum							stop							trap						

Other Information

Sentences

The words 'me' and 'of' will be introduced. They are not phonic but they are easily learned.

Coach

Ask the student to read the sentences. If all the words are read correctly tick the box.

1. Underline any words in a sentence which have not been read correctly and coach them.

2. After a period of **not less** than twenty-four hours you must ask the student to attempt the underlined words once more. When the student knows the word put a bar (/) through the underline with a pencil.

3. Tick the box when all the underlined words in a sentence have been barred. Dates are not required. However, you must keep returning to the underlined words until all boxes have been ticked.

The full sentence needs to be read once only but the underlined words must then be coached.

Never bar a word on the day that you coach it.

The big skip is full of mud so we can tell the girl to press it.

Who put the pet dog in the shed with the ram and the fat cat?

Why do you plot to swim in the tub with the frog but not the fish?

The girl was glad that Pat and Fred did not slip on the wet path.

What did you do before you came and ran with Pat in the hot sun?

Why have you put the thin frog with a fat leg in the tin bath?

Can you come and run with me to the bottom of the garden?

The brat had a bad plan so you can hit the top of the big drum.

Was the girl who came before Ann sad or glad?

Why does Jim put pins in a jar and who came here before Tom?

If you drill the flap we will have to trap the flex and the job will stop.

Do we mix the wet mud before we sell it to the girl on the hill?

Bob fled to the fells with a bag of cash on the top of his hat.

Does the bus come here for the man and does it run on petrol?

If you drip a hot drop on the tip of a spot who will stop the rot?

Check any previously completed grids for words which have not earned three ticks in a row.

Other Information

More Real Words with Initial Blends

Blends and simple words have been mixed in order to stop the student from pre-empting the sounds. We need the student to look at and build each word.

People with reading difficulties have a tendency to form blends spontaneously. The word 'bag' will be read as 'brag' without any apparent reason. Once a student forms an attachment to a non-existent blend, it is very difficult to remove. If asked to repeat the word, without guidance, a student will presume that there is some other error and compound the mistake.

As a student's word building skills develop the mistakes will become less frequent. The context will begin to point towards the sense and sound of words. We call the 's' at the end '**final s**' because it serves no purpose to differentiate between tense changes and plurals.

Coach

Your student should be familiar with initial blends and should be able to work through the grid in the usual way. However, this exercise will prove a little more tricky than the others because of the combination of simple words and words containing initial blends. You must correct mistakes as early as possible.

Your student may insert blends which are not there. Make sure you point out the error. If the student has difficulty with the **s** at the end of a word, ask him/her to read the word without it and then simply add **s** to the end.

You may take a word from the grid and demonstrate adding the **s** on scrap paper but remember to put a dot in the grid.

Some students may have to slow down a little with this exercise. It is not a time trial. Tick or dot the grid in the usual way with the usual twenty-four hour interval between attempts.

Day						Day						Day						Day					
Month						Month						Month						Month					
fits						top						had						swigs					
stags						plum						spit						blots					
wins						flops						grabs						clams					
pens						but						rib						drags					
traps						trams						lids						trill					
clips						trips						dogs						slid					
ten						let						grids						truss					
bug						stops						swim						drip					
crag						pot						frogs						dot					
bins						props						crags						flags					
drops						flats						puts						spill					
rugs						bun						flans						fans					
some						large						these						she					

Other Information

A Mixture of Skills

Sentences consolidate the work on a particular skill. We must establish, as early as possible, that negatives have to be worked on with the minimum period of twenty-four hours between attempts.

A student may know a word ten hours later but that does not mean a word is firmly established. We must give them time to loosen their grip on the word because it is the struggle to remember it that locks it into their long-term memory.

Coach

Ask the student to read the sentences. If all the words are read correctly tick the box.

1. Underline any words in a sentence which have not been read correctly and coach them.

2. After a period of **not less** than twenty-four hours you must ask the student to attempt the underlined words once more. When the student knows the word put a bar **(/)** through the underline with a pencil.

3. Tick the box when all the underlined words in a sentence have been barred. Dates are not required. However, you must keep returning to the underlined words until all boxes have been ticked.

The full sentence needs to be read once only but the underlined words must then be coached.

Never bar a word on the day that you coach it.

Some of them trap rats and have to run to the flats to sit on the bins.

These fat cats come here to run on the tops of the big tin sheds.

The pigs in the pen smell of rum and bad eggs.

Why do some of these men have cars and not vans?

Some of the fat hens on slabs sit on the large pot eggs.

Does the girl have a dog and did she feed it before she came here?

What shall we do before the dog and the pig run and jump on the grass?

She was here with the flags and not on the cliffs.

Do some of these rotten crops have large spots on top of black stems?

Put some of these rags in here with the dregs.

Why did she come to the top of the big cliff with Pat and not with me?

You will have to slap the lids to fit them on the large red cans.

The tins will be put in the shed with the large pots and pans.

She will have some of the large clams but not the large shells.

Other Information

Final Blends

People with reading difficulties will often focus on the area of a word which they find 'threatening'.

The final blend is an area which will dominate their attention, effectively stopping them from scanning the word from left to right in the normal manner.

Coach

Syllables and words are grouped in pairs. Ask the student to read the syllable first followed by the word.

Both syllable and paired word must be read correctly to earn a tick.

Make sure your student knows that these are real words. Each word needs to earn three consecutive ticks.

Each tick must be earned on a different day.

Tick the positives and dot the negatives.

Make sure you work on any negatives before you leave the page.

	Day											Day									
	Month											Month									
bon	bond										gran	grand									
cas	cast										graf	graft									
ten	tent										spen	spend									
san	sand										blas	blast									
lum	lump										craf	craft									
tas	task										cram	cramp									
pel	pelt										bran	brand									
bel	belt										clas	clasp									
mis	mist										twis	twist									
cos	cost										crus	crust									
fon	fond										tram	tramp									
lan	land										brin	brink									

Other Information

Initial & Final Blends

Coach

Make sure your student knows that these are real words.

Each word needs to earn three consecutive ticks.

Each tick must be earned on a different day.

Tick the positives and dot the negatives.

Make sure you work on any negatives before you leave the page.

Day								Day								Day								Day							
Month								Month								Month								Month							
crisp								frump								grant								tramp							
swank								brisk								trunk								clasp							
drunk								slump								spend								slink							
crank								drank								swift								splint							
blast								stunt								blend								stamp							
grasp								glint								frost								gland							
graft								brink								grunt								frank							
drift								spelt								clink								stump							
plank								frond								crust								blunt							
clamp								trust								twist								drink							
grand								stint								spent								think							
skunk								cramp								clank								stink							
her								or								go								their							

Other Information

Sentences

Once more the sentences have been deliberately constructed in an awkward manner. We cannot allow students to pre-empt the contents of a sentence. They must build words.

In later exercises, where the words are more complex, we will utilise the context to help students find the word.

Coach

Ask the student to read the sentences. If all the words are read correctly tick the box.

1. Underline any words in a sentence which have not been read correctly and coach them.

2. After a period of **not less** than twenty-four hours you must ask the student to attempt the underlined words once more. When the student knows the word put a bar **(/)** through the underline with a pencil.

3. Tick the box when all the underlined words in a sentence have been barred. Dates are not required. However, you must keep returning to the underlined words until all boxes have been ticked.

The full sentence needs to be read once only but the underlined words must then be coached.

Never bar a word on the day that you coach it.

Can their pet hen run as fast as their big dog?

Can we trust the tramp to grasp the hot crust before it rots?

The glass went clank as the fat man drank from the big flask.

If he tells her to jump she must hit the big drum with the tip of the staff.

Can Stella grab the plank with the big split or will she swim to the bank?

If we can get the lift we can go to the flats with Martin, Fred and Pat.

Brenda and Margaret, Dan and Amanda, came before Darren and Liz.

Grab the stump of the trunk and hit it with the large lump of rock.

She can trust the swift craft with the red mast but not the raft.

Mark and Frank have lost her disk so go and get the man with the plan.

Can you ask Jim if I left their melons and lemons with him or with Pam?

The bull lifts his horns and stamps on the thorns in the yard.

Mildred and Frank will get cramp if you push them on the wet path.

Step on the plank but not on the bank or you will crash on the ramp.

Other Information

Tongue Twisters

Most of our students, particularly the dyslexics, have trouble with initial blends. It seems that once they focus on a certain blend they tend to carry the sound into the word following.

This exercise is designed to make easier the transition from blend to blend.

Coach

All the words in a row must be read correctly to earn a tick. Dates are not required. Your student will find this a difficult but enjoyable exercise.

As soon as a negative is produced say **'stop'**. Dot the box and continue on the next line. Change the order of reading with each attempt. Work from the bottom line upwards or start with the last word first.

This is basically a fluency exercise and **none of the words are eligible for the multi-sensory grids.**

Your student may never earn three ticks. In such cases you must not allow him/her to become downhearted. If you promote the severity of this exercise your student will take up the challenge.

swill	wills	sills	swills
crop	prop	cop	crops
trap	taps	parts	spats
drip	dips	pip	drips
clamp	clan	camp	clams
split	slit	silt	stilts
stag	sags	gasp	gags
bran	ban	bans	barn
glad	garb	grab	brags
flog	fog	logs	golf
sniff	fins	sift	stiff
grid	grill	grip	glib
gums	glum	smug	mugs
strip	tips	pits	spits
blot	plot	pots	spots

Check any previously completed grids for words which have not earned three ticks in a row.

Other Information

Vowels & Consonants

The recognition of vowels is fundamental to syllable division.

This exercise is designed to stimulate the student's ability to recognise the vowels within a word. The configuration opposite gives appropriate nouns for the vowel sounds. These are the most commonly used images for expressing these sounds.

The stereotypical image of the American Indian is unfortunate. However, we need a noun which brings to mind quickly the letter sound 'i'. Children no longer recognise quills and ink bottles. The igloo too is less easily recognised and we could be accused of stereotyping Eskimos. The image may seem complicated but we know that it works - even with students who have severe problems.

Coach

Ask the student to study the picture on the opposite page.

You must tell him/her that it shows an apple **(a)** on an elephant's **(e)** tusk and an Indian **(i)** sitting on its back.

An orange **(o)** is stuck on the point of the umbrella **(u)** which the elephant is holding with its tail.

Your student must close his/her eyes and imagine the picture. Ask what s/he can see.

When the vowel sounds are known you may turn to the next exercise.

Remember! We still require the short sounds.

Other Information

Recognising Vowels

This exercise may seem easy to people whose lives are not blighted by reading problems. However, *we are* dealing with students who *do have* reading problems.

This exercise must be given the weight of consideration that it is due. Overlook it and you will be the architect of all manner of problems.

Coach

Using a pencil as a pointer, move along each line of letters, ask your student to say **yes** to the vowels and **no** to the other letters (consonants).

If s/he fails to make the distinction or misses a vowel, you must stop working with that line, dot the grid and move to the next line.

Difficulties can be overcome by referring, once more, to the apple/elephant/…etc on the previous page.

The 'three tick rule' applies.

It may seem simple but this exercise is very important. Do not overlook this or any other exercise.

Day									Day								
Month									Month								

A

milugtipnba								
roitleparstr								
brupdtnikom								
quilkmoiner								
scroaptimkl								
arecdztpswr								
dranssupein								
cradfuimeok								

B

ujitrewskjgf								
lkmrewaqujk								
lakfewuopmb								
cxzduiplojhg								
afeolertukvc								
inmiokesajb								
aeikmnhousi								
mijhoaexujld								

Coach: Work on column A only. Use column B if your student fails to earn three ticks in a row in column A

Other Information

Introducing 'Polynons' & Syllable Division

The term 'Polynons' describes words which are both polysyllabic and meaningless. Their only function is to serve the needs of word-building and syllable division.

Syllable division must be a multi-sensory activity; requiring students to divide words physically with a pencil stroke before they can undertake the reading of polysyllabic words.

Coach

Look at the words in the shaded area of the exercise.

The words have been divided according to **Toe by Toe's** rules for syllable division. The rule is: Starting from the left, look for the first vowel, take the consonant to the right of it and divide. Twin consonants count as one letter.

The Polynons in the shaded area are examples only. **Make sure that your student works in the unshaded columns on the right**.

Ask the student to draw the dividing lines with a pencil. You may have to rub out the lines until the student becomes familiar with the rules.

This is not a reading exercise. Dividing the Polynons is all that is required.

This is an important exercise which will be expanded later. It seems more complex than it is.

It may help you to copy some of the polynons on to scrap paper and attempt to divide them yourself.

Dates are not required but you must keep returning to the exercise until the student knows how to divide correctly.

Column 1	Column 2
Examples of syllable division Note: twin consonants count as one letter	The rule is: find the consonant after the vowel and divide. Use a pencil.

Column 1		Column 2	
cran/tip/at	fenn/am/an	plettonsig	grepsannat
han/pes/tot	att/im/sap	attifsad	dipsaff
fram/gop/dom	crebb/en/tip	cremstin	naddemop
ban/dig/dop	or/tigg/op	drogplat	gladdemop
star/grim/on	sudd/om/en	flettonit	nittemox
bras/ken/mip	app/dimm/on	oppendig	axitripp
ed/pon/tin	sligg/an/det	pressopag	ixammix
in/trim/stip	cliff/tapp/on	lippenfonn	sacrimat
slip/un/gap	grimm/ad/ot	rensaftip	rodiggat
ar/im/es/top	ox/im/ogg/tip	astoppet	mandobat
club/on/frit	prodd/an/im	cabsomsin	crandimm
swin/kon/lip	or/dinn/am	lettobsun	Loggintop

Other Information

The Long and Short Sound of Vowels and the Mute 'e'

The ability to switch quickly between the long and short vowel sounds is essential to good word-building.

We use the terms 'long and 'short' sound of vowels instead of the 'name' and 'sound' because it better describes how the sound differs when a distinction has to be made. The mute 'e' elongates the sound. Listen to the example in the coaching box.

Coach

The shaded areas in the first two columns invite the coach to ask the student for the sound of the vowel opposite the words **long** or **short.**

The coach must point to the letter and ask for the long or short sound as directed.

In the third column the long or short sound of the vowel is decided by the presence or absence of the letter **e** at the end of the word.

The letter **e** at the end of the word is the same as having the word **long** in the shaded area.

Example: **at** - put on the silent (mute) **e** and the word becomes **ate**.

Day										Day										Day									
Month										Month										Mth									
short	a									long	u									ap									
long	e									short	a									ape									
short	i									short	e									ud									
short	o									short	i									ude									
long	u									long	a									at									
short	a									short	u									ate									
short	e									long	o									im									
long	u									long	i									ime									
long	o									short	e									ob									
short	i									long	a									obe									
long	a									short	i									it									

Other Information

Mute 'e' Nonsense Words

In order to stop the student from anticipating sounds we have mixed the mute 'e' words with others that carry the short sound.

Coach

This is the sequel to the previous exercise.

Ask the student to listen to the way that the word **rat** turns to **rate** when we add the mute **e**. Initially, you will have to remind your student constantly of the power of the mute **e** and how it changes the vowel before it.

These nonsense words need to earn three consecutive ticks.

Each tick must be earned on a different day.

Tick the positives and dot the negatives.

Coach the negatives as soon as they occur and make sure you work on them once more before you leave the page.

You must make sure that you take the **first** answer and dot or tick accordingly. Do not accept that your student has just been careless.

Day						
Month						
tume						
con						
dese						
pef						
sidd						
nipe						
lote						
sade						
sote						
labb						
pof						
mofe						

Day						
Month						
tofe						
sate						
rabe						
tane						
bezz						
ribe						
rux						
mife						
tobe						
gafe						
vone						
fise						

Day						
Month						
tud						
ren						
gute						
gobe						
teb						
sabe						
hane						
fofe						
cass						
tiss						
pite						
mafe						

Day						
Month						
ene						
leb						
rofe						
pid						
bep						
boke						
pime						
tib						
sone						
bine						
tet						
hom						

Other Information

Real Words

Coach

Make sure your student knows that these are real words.

Each word needs to earn three consecutive ticks.

Each tick must be earned on a different day.

Tick the positives and dot the negatives.

Make sure you work on any negatives before you leave the page.

This exercise is three pages long.

The last page contains words with **s** on the end. Make sure that your student understands that the rule for the **mute e** still applies.

Day									Day									Day								
Month									Month									Month								
ride									pin									late								
pot									tile									hot								
hope									fan									hide								
yes									dig									rope								
dole									dope									set								
fin									sit									cave								
rat									wide									tone								
site									rife									got								
mate									bag									ripe								
lone									bone									jig								
log									hate									bun								
when									over									bring								

Day		Day		Day	
Month		Month		Month	
pane		lime		dip	
did		home		dope	
nod		pit		life	
fade		fad		sad	
lot		cane		lag	
pad		rise		gale	
note		cog		pod	
pile		tune		pole	
tag		rum		tap	
run		sum		sale	
vet		fit		tape	
each		use		want	

Day										Day										Day									
Month										Month										Month									

Remind the student that the mute 'e' rule still applies to the words with 's' at the end.

domes							sides							soles		
Dan							Ron							pip		
lame							rile							lines		
Bill							Meg							Sam		
dame							file							wine		
Tom							Sid							Kim		
same							dates							dine		
Tim							Bob							Ben		
fame							ale							pines		
Pat							Rob							Ann		
tame							pale							fine		

Other Information

Sentences

Coach

Ask the student to read the sentences. If all the words are read correctly tick the box.

1. Underline any words in a sentence which have not been read correctly and coach them.

2. After a period of **not less** than twenty-four hours you must ask the student to attempt the underlined words once more. When the student knows the word put a bar **(/)** through the underline with a pencil.

3. Tick the box when all the underlined words in a sentence have been barred. Dates are not required. However, you must keep returning to the underlined words until all boxes have been ticked.

The full sentence needs to be read once only but the underlined words must then be coached.

Never bar a word on the day that you coach it.

You must take each case on its merit and forget the rest.

Use the taxi if you want Belinda to bring the box home.

Tell some of these jokes to the sad blokes from the North.

When will you fill each of these holes with tar and stones?

Martha and Pamela had to cope with a difficult problem.

The men who came up from the mines lost their jobs.

The land will be safe if you put stakes before the gates.

You must spend more if you want a big glass of lemonade.

Kate left the rides to run and jump over the big stones.

Some children take the brakes from prams and make a mess.

He made some pancakes on top of the stove before he came.

I can bring cash or use the card if I want to shop in the sales.

Drive the car over the hills then take a bus to the market.

Use a rope when you scale a cliff and tie the line to a rock.

Other Information

Mute 'e' Nonsense Words

This exercise has been extended to three pages because it is vital that we extend and consolidate a student's ability to move quickly between the long and short sound of vowels.

Words without the mute 'e' have been inserted in order to stop the student pre-empting the long sound of the vowel. The student must look at the word and build it.

Coach

Make sure your student knows that these are nonsense words. Ask him/her to beware of words without the mute **e**.

Each word needs to earn three consecutive ticks.

Each tick must be earned on a different day.

Tick the positives and dot the negatives.

Make sure you work on any negatives before you leave the page.

This exercise continues for three pages.

Before you start!
Remind your student that the **e** on the end of a word gives the preceding vowel its long sound.

Day							
Month							
spafe							
clat							
trine							
glite							
stilf							
grome							
stap							
fraxon							
clibe							
prape							

Day							
Month							
flate							
stise							
glode							
clise							
swike							
slup							
cline							
drope							
grafe							
clote							

Day							
Month							
skude							
shabe							
swiff							
frine							
prote							
glame							
drid							
brose							
crote							
slafe							

Day										
Month										
grife										
frat										
slame										
drobe										
grame										
drant										
slame										
glim										
prabe										
dripe										

Day										
Month										
frote										
drame										
floke										
glafe										
groff										
drine										
droke										
clipe										
stape										
sloke										

Day										
Month										
broze										
spult										
spile										
thrat										
strite										
shripe										
sprate										
thrime										
strabe										
thrate										

Day								
Month								
flase								
tropp								
stame								
skite								
brone								
clase								
trafe								
glate								
grite								
spod								

Day								
Month								
trife								
swide								
stope								
flike								
snitt								
spone								
trith								
glane								
flepe								
stafe								

Day								
Month								
glabe								
glode								
trofe								
brape								
stome								
stibbix								
clope								
glone								
clate								
crine								

Other Information

Real Words Using Initial Blends and Mute 'e'

There may be some debate over the inclusion of **blue** / **glue** / **clue**. However, the letters **ue** can be pronounced in many different ways and we would prefer to place it amongst the **mute 'e'** category for convenience. The sound made by the **ue** is different but not so distinctly different that it cannot be learned quickly.

Coach

Make sure your student knows that these are real words.

Each word needs to earn three consecutive ticks.

Each tick must be earned on a different day.

Tick the positives and dot the negatives.

Make sure you work on any negatives before you leave the page.

Some words have **S** on the end. Your student should know that the **mute e** rule still applies to these words.

Help may be needed with the words **blue**, **true** and **glue**.

Day		Day		Day	
Month		Month		Month	
crones		grime		slime	
blame		blade		probe	
grades		groves		flakes	
spoke		skate		pride	
true		clue		blue	
stiles		bride		stoves	
crave		grape		drape	
drove		spines		staves	
glade		slate		grates	
tripe		glide		crimes	
slaves		crates		swore	
be		new		may	

Other Information

Sentences

Coach

Ask the student to read the sentences. If all the words are read correctly tick the box.

1. Underline any words in a sentence which have not been read correctly and coach them.

2. After a period of **not less** than twenty-four hours you must ask the student to attempt the underlined words once more. When the student knows the word put a bar (/) through the underline with a pencil.

3. Tick the box when all the underlined words in a sentence have been barred. Dates are not required. However, you must keep returning to the underlined words until all boxes have been ticked.

The full sentence needs to be read once only but the underlined words must then be coached.

Never bar a word on the day that you coach it.

Take some flakes and bake some cakes before Steve arrives in the kitchen.

The dark glade was full of men from Rome who came to attack the tribe.

You may cut grapes and a date with a sharp blade made from bone and flint.

She stole the new dress before she went home and gave the buttons to Dave.

May I drink the wine then flake and grate some dates on the plate?

Smile with pride at the bride as she drives to the chapel with Dad at her side.

Slides and fast rides can make some children and adults sick.

Is the girl brave and will she skate on the drive with you and Clive?

Who can state if the time is late and do you want to bake a cake for Mum?

Be brave and hit the snake that sits on the grass with the big stone.

The new times can make some men late but not those who go home on a bus.

You will be home in time if you go before it gets dark over the hills in the West.

Do not drive the car if the brakes will not stop it before the bottom of the hill.

Push with the spade and dig up some swedes, parsnips and carrots.

Check any previously completed grids for words which have not earned three ticks in a row.

Other Information

Nonsense Words Using the Digraphs 'ay' & 'oy'

Vowels and digraph sounds are subject to regional variations.

Parents will have little difficulty in teaching their children but teachers from 'out of town' should be aware of all the nuances of local pronunciation.

Coach

Make sure your student knows that these are nonsense words.

Explain to your student that **ay** makes the sound **ay** as in **may** and **oy** makes the **oy** sound as in **boy**.

Take the first answer and tick or dot.

Each word needs to earn three consecutive ticks.

Each tick must be earned on a different day.

Tick the positives and dot the negatives.

Make sure you work on any negatives before you leave the page.

Day						
Month						

oy	goy	blay
ay	shoy	floy
oy	loy	skoy
ay	soy	skay
oy	vay	glay
oy	voy	broy
hoy	zay	droy
ay	tay	chay
poy	cay	choy
oy	spay	shay
noy	croy	smoy
nay	stoy	cloy

Other Information

Real Words

Coach

Make sure your student knows that these are real words.

Each word needs to earn three consecutive ticks.

Each tick must be earned on a different day.

Tick the positives and dot the negatives.

Make sure you work on any negatives before you leave the page.

Day								Day								Day							
Month								Month								Month							
Roy								jays								brays							
coy								rays								sways							
say								may								rayon							
toy								boys								crayon							
bay								pays								display							
hay								pray								sprays							
day								clay								affray							
boy								slay								dismay							
way								ploy								strays							
lay								fray								soya							
Kay								play								Moyra							
your								walk								are							

Other Information

Sentences

Coach

Ask the student to read the sentences. If all the words are read correctly tick the box.

1. Underline any words in a sentence which have not been read correctly and coach them.

2. After a period of **not less** than twenty-four hours you must ask the student to attempt the underlined words once more. When the student knows the word put a bar **(/)** through the underline with a pencil.

3. Tick the box when all the underlined words in a sentence have been barred. Dates are not required. However, you must keep returning to the underlined words until all boxes have been ticked.

The full sentence needs to be read once only but the underlined words must then be coached.

Never bar a word on the day that you coach it.

Will Ray walk or can he travel with his dad on the bus on Sundays?

Your boys are joyful and playful on Mondays when we play with clay on a tray.

Pay for a tray of crayfish and send it to Roy before Monday.

Bake the clay and make Ray pay for the toys and models.

Is it true that, on hot days in May, your royal hens lay eggs in the hay?

If you do not stay close to the bay you will be swept away on the tide.

He came from far away to play here but did not stay till the end of the day.

Who is Moyra and did she pay to stay before she left to go home for the day?

Is it true that jays in May make nests from clay and do the boys like saveloys?

You are not to walk home with May and Ray but you can play with your toys.

Do the boys and girls play with the sticky clay and who can stay for the day?

Are the boys with Roya and is she the girl from Iran?

Did he say I am a royal boy or did he say I am a loyal boy?

Ann and Steve will not walk with the girl who is a loyal royalist.

Other Information

Polynons and the Sounds: 'th' 'ch' 'sh'

Toe by Toe syllable division is vital for reading polysyllabic words. It may seem tedious but it works.

Toe by Toe word building is part of a structured **working** system. Using this method, the authors teach children and adults, including the severely dyslexic, and obtain unparalleled results.

Coach

The exercise on page **63** introduced **polynons** and **Toe by Toe** syllable division. Working from left to right, the rule is: **find the consonant after the first vowel and divide.** Twin consonants are counted as one therefore your student should divide after the double letters: e.g: **ff/ ss/ tt/.**

The same rules apply to this exercise but we need to expand it. The letter **h** within the polynon must not be divided from the letter before it. In other words, the divide must come after the sounds of
ch/ sh/ th/.

The shaded area has examples to help you. Remember this is not a reading exercise. Ask the student to use a pencil to draw the dividing lines. You may have to erase them until the student becomes familiar with the rules.

Do not think for one moment that you can overlook this exercise. It is a vital step towards reading longer and more complex words. Overlook this exercise or any other and you will seriously hinder your student's progress.

Examples of syllable division	Remember the rule: Find the consonant after the vowel and include the 'h'.

Examples only		**Divide only - do not read**	
brash/ath/om	Bass/ach/oy	redashop	chippunox
chap/ash/ill	chap/ash/oll	thrannox	skanishom
nogg/ash	oth/ash/ap	oshimatt	staggibad
clutt/ar/oy	brath/pin	grushdog	climmopad
dibb/on/op	mash/ip/ay	ussachim	drishattay
mash/ip/ad	ath/an/od	tumathix	thubbenox
ith/an/od	math/an/oss	nummenog	hachinniff
daff/el/en	tach/ass/om	ishiffax	bishathizz
clath/opp/id	ith/ax/ad/ox	grundigop	tishamiff
drash/ton/im	chim/add/im	athinop	grafticat
cush/ith/op	frash/toll/ad	trashbop	brimmon
fumm/ich/ip	bleth/tip	ordinax	thunndom

Other Information

More syllable division using 'ck'

Students have already been introduced to '**ck**' but we need to expand the range of usage to longer words. Students regard these exercises as a change from the routine and usually enjoy them.

The real virtue of the exercise will not be realized until the student is introduced to the longer words in the later exercises.

Coach

You should now be familiar with the rules of syllable division.
They apply to this exercise but we have expanded them to involve the letters **ck**.

Never divide the letters **ck**.

We have given you plenty of examples.

Ask your student to use a pencil to divide the Polynons.

Don't forget!
This is not a reading exercise.

Below are examples of syllable division which now involve 'ck'	Ask the student to divide the polynons below. Remind them of the rules.
Examples only	**Do not read**

black/in/ash	back/on/tip	s k i n n i m i n	t u c k i n n o p
chigg/ax	ish/ap/top	t r i c k a n n o t	s l i s h o d d e n
dash/ack/im	ax/im/ax/im	s c o f f a b u d	c h i p p i n t i s h
stash/ock	track/obb/an	t i c k a n n i t	s h a c k i m u t h
bick/om/ish	iss/op/ick	d i g g a s h u d	t r i m m o l l
trash/ath/ox	chadd/ick	c l i c k i t t a p	a r n i c k o m
oth/ick/oll	shimm/ick	m e n t a n n e t	d e l l i m m o n
lith/em/ick	thim/tish	t o p p i n n i s h	s u l l i b a n
ack/in/ath	edd/as/tock	c l a p p a n i t h	c a d d i n n i s h
bish/eff/an	tripp/ick	l i c k o d d o t	t r a m m i c k
ox/ick/om	stam/tish	s t i m t i g g a n	c o m m o c k
hick/ip/ash	glas/timm/uck	d o t h a f f a s h	l i m m i s h

Other Information

Nonsense words using the sound of: 'ch' & 'tch'

The '**t**' before the '**ch**' regulates the sound of the preceding vowel which will always take the short sound.

Nonsense words make students build words and, once more, we have mixed the skills in order to stop them from pre-empting the sounds. We need your student to look at the entire word.

Coach

Make sure that your student knows that these are nonsense words.

Tell the student that a **t** before a **ch** is silent. It must be ignored. The sound created by **tch** is the same as **ch** for **ch**ip.

When your student reads nonsense words you may accept either the soft or the hard sound of the letters **th**.

Each word needs to earn three consecutive ticks.

Each tick must be earned on a different day.

Tick the positives and dot the negatives.

Make sure you work on any negatives before you leave the page.

Day										
Month										
thep										
shim										
chep										
shan										
shib										
shup										
sitch										
setch										
mish										
noth										

Day										
Month										
feth										
nith										
lith										
coth										
drith										
brotch										
bleth										
wetch										
swith										
chim										

Day										
Month										
chup										
pith										
chon										
shif										
rith										
fatch										
crith										
fash										
frith										
desh										

Other Information

More nonsense words

This is a simple exercise and your student should not experience too much difficulty.

We could point out in the coaching box that the letters **'ck'** always denote that any vowel preceding them carries the short sound but that would mean the introduction of another rule.

Rules will be introduced but we must endeavour to keep them to a minimum.

Coach

Make sure your student knows that these are nonsense words.

Remind the student that **ck** makes the single sound of the letter **c** as in **car**.

Each word needs to earn three consecutive ticks.

Each tick must be earned on a different day.

Tick the positives and dot the negatives.

Make sure you work on any negatives before you leave the page.

Day										
Month										
brock										
feck										
slock										
grick										
trock										
fack										
zick										
cleck										
frack										
smick										

Day										
Month										
smuck										
grock										
plock										
sleck										
dreck										
creck										
jick										
smeck										
glack										
pock										

Day										
Month										
bleck										
greck										
preck										
gleck										
prack										
dack										
skick										
teck										
drick										
pleck										

Other Information

Revision of 'th' 'sh' 'ch' 'ck'

The words have been paired to sharpen the student's ability to make the distinction between the above sounds.

Coach

Make sure your student knows that these are real words.

The words have been paired and both words must be read correctly to earn a tick.

Each pair needs to earn three consecutive ticks.

Each tick must be earned on a different day.

Tick the positives and dot the negatives.

Make sure you work on any negatives before you leave the page.

	Day												Day										
	Month												Month										
sash	rush											speck	crock										
gush	rack											frock	brick										
dish	such											trash	pitch										
pick	lock											sick	pack										
lash	posh											froth	ditch										
luck	push											clock	cloth										
dash	mash											clash	thick										
neck	crack											cluck	rash										
thin	black											tack	gash										
rich	path											tick	duck										
lick	slick											flush	clutch										
flash	stack											snack	patch										
small	tall											too	said										

Other Information

Sentences

Coach

Ask the student to read the sentences. If all the words are read correctly tick the box.

1. Underline any words in a sentence which have not been read correctly and coach them.

2. After a period of **not less** than twenty-four hours you must ask the student to attempt the underlined words once more. When the student knows the word put a bar (/) through the underline with a pencil.

3. Tick the box when all the underlined words in a sentence have been barred. Dates are not required. However, you must keep returning to the underlined words until all boxes have been ticked.

The full sentence needs to be read once only but the underlined words must then be coached.

Never bar a word on the day that you coach it.

Who is the tall boy with the small blue bike and did he ride or walk up the hill?

The small boy said nothing to the tall girl but he spoke quite a lot to his mum.

May I check the locks before it gets too late and when can I bring them over?

The thick stick is on the black shelf and the thin girl stands next to the drum.

Close to the dish, a duck sits on the patch as the man with the dog walks away.

A rich boy with a limp cannot walk to the bank with his hands in his pockets.

The dock is posh so take a fish home and bring the dog to the side of the path.

Dash to the pitch to catch the hat before it gets too dark in the stand.

"If you crash you may get a stiff neck," said the tall man with the big nose.

"Put the mash with some hash," said Jim, "and bring me some milk in a glass."

Go to the hills and bring back some fat to trap the rats and make a slide for me.

Over the hills and far away she made a fat pack from thin black cloth.

Pack the bag with thick sticks and stack a box of tacks on top of the mats.

Take the truck to the docks for a crate of fish but do not bring back a haddock.

Pass the dish of frogs legs to Fred and then pass them in a bucket to Jake.

Check any previously completed grids for words which have not earned three ticks in a row.

Other Information

The letter 'y' at the end of a word

The letter **'y'** can take either the long or the short sound of the letter **'i'** at the end of a word.

This may seem obvious to most observers of the printed word but it can be a source of confusion to people with reading problems.

Coach

Make sure your student knows that these are real words.

A mixture of skills is needed for this exercise. The words in the first part of the exercise with **y** endings carry the sound of the letter **y** as in **Billy**.

In the second part of the exercise the **y** at the end will carry the long sound as in the word **fly**.

The words have been paired and both words must be read correctly to earn a tick.

Each pair needs to earn three consecutive ticks.

Each tick must be earned on a different day.

Tick the positives and dot the negatives.

Make sure you work on any negatives before you leave the page.

Most problems in this exercise will be caused by the student giving the wrong sound to the final y.
In such cases, ask your student to switch the sounds of the last letter.

Remember: A coached word earns a dot.

Day		Day	
Month		Month	

Short sound

happy	hungry		spry	satisfy	
holly	frisky		kilt	rely	
vest	jolly		verify	fist	
daft	test		try	end	
lily	madly		best	grand	
Polly	Billy		testify	dry	
bulky	just		dent	mend	
silly	hint		fry	edify	
thrill	candy		went	list	
class	brandy		sly	cry	
Kitty	misty		fly	from	
all	don't		gone	most	

Long sound

Other Information

Sentences

Coach

Ask the student to read the sentences. If all the words are read correctly tick the box.

1. Underline any words in a sentence which have not been read correctly and coach them.

2. After a period of **not less** than twenty-four hours you must ask the student to attempt the underlined words once more. When the student knows the word put a bar **(/)** through the underline with a pencil.

3. Tick the box when all the underlined words in a sentence have been barred. Dates are not required. However, you must keep returning to the underlined words until all boxes have been ticked.

The full sentence needs to be read once only but the underlined words must then be coached.

Never bar a word on the day that you coach it.

The short sound of 'y' at the end of a word.

Gone are the days when most men drank frothy ale every day.

Can you tell Andy and Sally to go to the park with Jimmy and Samantha?

Daddy can tell all of you a funny story but not if he is angry or unwell.

Milly said that the drink was too fizzy for Tommy and Jimmy.

The sherry was on the tray with the milk, cakes and wobbly jelly.

Don't let the silly children play with the brolly when it is wet and windy.

Twenty men drank most of the milk and ate all of the royal jelly.

Lemonade may get up your nose if you drink it too quickly.

Tommy was very unhappy when the puppy ate the soggy socks.

Don't copy the notes and tell me if Jimmy is happy or sad.

Bring some wet clay and I will bake some very hard bricks but not today.

Does the frilly dress come from the shop or did you make it?

Take most of the raspberry jam and tell me if the pasty has gone from the shelf.

Plenty of chips and plenty of fish make me very happy.

Other Information

Sentences

Coach

Ask the student to read the sentences. If all the words are read correctly tick the box.

Point out that **y** in the middle of a word can take the long sound e.g. fl**y**ing st**y**le

Remember to apply the skills for reading ay / oy

1. Underline any words in a sentence which have not been read correctly and coach them.

2. After a period of **not less** than twenty-four hours you must ask the student to attempt the underlined words once more. When the student knows the word put a bar **(/)** through the underline with a pencil.

3. Tick the box when all the underlined words in a sentence have been barred. Dates are not required. However, you must keep returning to the underlined words until all boxes have been ticked.

The full sentence needs to be read once only but the underlined words must then be coached.

Never bar a word on the day that you coach it.

The long sound of 'y' at the end and in the middle of a word.

"Why does my large chicken try to fry big fat chips in the pig sty?" said Myra.

The boy with the empty glass must try not to cry over the spilt milk.

All of the fish swam away and most of the men have gone home to get dry.

Try not to terrify or horrify the shy man with the hybrid rose in his button hole.

Don't apply for the job if you cannot satisfy the man who brings the forms.

Supply all the boys with a pan and some fat to fry the chops.

Testify that most of the hybrid plants are not in small red pots.

Stand by the red hydrant and watch the firemen quell the flames.

Can you go to the Clyde and jump off the plank and make a splash?

I think that her stylish pal was a spy for most of his adult life.

Fortify the wine with spirits and magnify the print with the bottom of a glass.

You can edify the class with some tales of the past and present.

The tall man has gone to develop the film but most of the small men are here.

Drop me a line in July, not in March, when it is still too wet to walk on the grass.

If you stray away from the path you will probably slip on the wet mud.

Other Information

A Mixture of Skills

This exercise has been designed to consolidate the student's new word building skills.

The letter 'a' in the word 'solitary' and the letter 'o' in the word 'bishop' are unstressed. We could introduce any number of rules to deal with unstressed letters or letters which take on a different sound according to their proximity to other letters but we need to keep the system as uncomplicated as possible.

Coach

Ask the student to read the sentences. If all the words are read correctly tick the box.

1. Underline any words in a sentence which have not been read correctly and coach them.

2. After a period of **not less** than twenty-four hours you must ask the student to attempt the underlined words once more. When the student knows the word put a bar (/) through the underline with a pencil.

3. Tick the box when all the underlined words in a sentence have been barred. Dates are not required. However, you must keep returning to the underlined words until all boxes have been ticked.

The full sentence needs to be read once only but the underlined words must then be coached. Most problems arising from this exercise can be easily dealt with by switching from the long to the short sound of **y** or vice versa.

Never bar a word on the day that you coach it.

Inspire the girl to fulfil her desire but do not be too sympathetic.

All of the girls went for a walk before most of the boys woke up.

Robin's men ate the Sheriff's venison and then drank his best Burgundy wine.

Take the ferry across the lake and carry the dish of jelly for your mum.

In some parts of Canada the land is dry but chilly in the month of May.

"I think it would be folly for the bishop to sing that song with Molly," said Fred.

Clarify, verify and testify if you must but try not to mystify or horrify the witness.

"Put the soggy mats on the line and put the hose-pipe away," said Erica.

"I suppose you must think that I have gone quite mad," said Veronica.

The solitary man spent his salary on jam and ate lots of spaghetti on Sunday.

"Don't cry for the rest of the day or you will make all of us sad," said Henry.

If you walk too far the bus may have gone before you get home.

"We will be in time for the birthday party if you don't delay the bus," said Janet.

Send the bully down the line and make him testify that he is bad.

It was his vanity and not insanity which made the boy so nasty and silly.

I cannot deny that I did defy most of the tall lads from across the Atlantic.

Other Information

More Syllable Division

The letter **'h'** in the English language is often unaspirated at the beginning of a word. Within a word, **'h'** usually forms part of a digraph.

Coach

This is a normal syllable division exercise. The basic rules are the same. Ask the student to find the consonant following the vowel and draw the line after it. However, the rule has been expanded once more:

Do not divide the letters **tch**.
Do not split the **mute e** from the end of a polynon.

We do not need a line at the end of a polynon.

Wrong	Correct
at/chape	atch/ape
is/hen	ish/en
at/hone	ath/one
on/net	onn/et
ic/ktime	ick/time

In the shaded area you will find more completed polynons to help you.

Remember! This is not a reading exercise.

Examples of syllable division	Do not split a **'t'** from **'ch'** and never split the mute **'e'** from the rest of the polynon.

Divide the polynons below

mitch/ome	scrumm/ode	t i s h o p l o d e	d i t h i c h i n e
ip/att/ane	shoth/an/ope	n i t c h o p a s h	r o c k i t c h
dif/atch/ofe	iss/im/ach	r i c k a s h o n	a p p o d s i t c h
ship/itch	ack/egg/ape	o b m i t c h o f e	g a n n i p i n e
chatt/om/itch	poll/utch/opp	p a t h a n o c k	d a t c h e m u p
in/thetch/og	tick/un/date	r i s h o m a t	f r i t c h i p o d e
framm/ill	blogg/ann/ock	c l a s h o m e	s h u m t i p a n e
sutch/ope	thor/nick/oll	g l i b b o m i c k	c h o c k t i m e
datch/um	trapp/ab/ite	d i t h a c k o t e	s o y a p o d e
frish/ope	slugg/ax	v i c k o m a t	l o t c h e r f i t e
chonn/at/ick	bagg/as/tope	c l i p a c k i l e	d i m m i s h o f f
glapp/it/back	shimm/ad/ock	c h a t t o x	p i l t e m m i s h

Other Information

Reading Polynons

Unlike the previous exercise, the emphasis here is on reading rather than syllable division. We need to cultivate a more flowing approach to polynons with syllable division becoming a mental rather than a physical skill.

Having divided them, students will be familiar with half of the polynons on the exercise page. Now they must read them.

Initially, without a context to help them and without any indication of stresses, some students will struggle to read the polynons correctly.

However, our interest lies in the student's ability to activate the skills that they have been taught in the previous exercises. We can afford to be less stringent with the rules and allow for two positive answers. *Real words* will always require three consecutive ticks.

Coach

Ask the student to read the polynons on the opposite page. When a polynon has been read correctly you must tick the first box.

Dots and dates are not needed.

The other box can be ticked when the polynon has been read correctly on another occasion.

If your student has difficulty, ask him/her to read the polynon syllable by syllable, using the skills developed in the syllable division exercises.

Ask your student to divide them in his/her head. A pencil should not be used. It may be helpful to move a piece of card along the polynon - stopping at the syllable divisions.

Read

bannashine

justachip

tishopmode

nitchopash

rickashon

obmitchofe

glibbomick

dithacote

vickammate

clippimmone

chattox

amitchock

appodsitch

rockitch

Read

itchipone

lappitane

gannipine

datchimup

fritchipode

shumtiplane

chocktime

soyaspode

lotcherfite

dimmishoff

piltemmish

mitchome

ippattane

difatchome

Read

cratchimmat

mackindite

shippitch

chattomitch

inthetchog

frammill

sutchope

chonnatick

clappitback

scrummode

shothanope

issinnatch

ackeggape

pollutchop

Other Information

Revision of some word building skills

Revision is not an optional extra. The coach must consolidate the student's newly acquired word building skills.

Coach

This is a simple but nevertheless important revision exercise. Both words in a pair need to be read correctly to earn a tick.

Make sure your student knows that these are real words. Each pair of words needs to earn three consecutive ticks.

Each tick must be earned on a different day.

Tick the positives and dot the negatives.

Make sure you work on any negatives before you leave the page.

	Day									
	Month									
press	limes									
drink	chaps									
wind	timid									
rakes	smell									
bones	wakes									
match	catch									
grunt	smack									
rose	blot									
glad	spills									
twins	flame									
latch	skin									
they	find									

	Day									
	Month									
carp	swill									
pack	mask									
tandem	cracks									
glen	clank									
taste	zest									
use	parade									
pitch	ripe									
ditch	clash									
twitch	stuck									
twist	silly									
tape	smile									
could	women									

Other Information

More Revision

Could the women from the West consume all the cakes?

The women from the North could not find their way home.

Hatch an egg by the hot stove and drink a glass of milk.

Find some spines and twigs and make a nest for the ducks on the lake.

If they come to the fort you must fly a black flag on the top of the hill.

Trim the hot tripe with a sharp blade but do not scratch your hand.

Some tramps and brave women catch fish in the lake.

Did the Swedes hide in the wet ditch or did they catch the bus?

Hot flames and hot ovens can char the currant buns and rock cakes.

Black spots can often drip on the mat if you forget to wipe your hands.

Before we could stop them they had left their bags and gone home.

In this shop the big clock is often fast but not on Sundays.

We will have to decorate each new kitchen with small red tiles.

Who said that the black witch from the dark forest ate bats?

"All of the men and women could fit on the small bus," said Sandra.

Other Information

Syllable division introducing 'er' & 'ing' endings

Pronunciation always causes problems for students with reading difficulties and polynons are extremely difficult for some students to 'spit out'.

However, we need them to look at the structure of words irrespective of their capacity to pronounce them. As the words grow longer, these exercises will become increasingly important.

Coach

This exercise deals with words which end in **er** or **ing**. Ask your student to listen to the sounds made by the bold endings of the following words:

runn**ing**   broth**er**.

The **ing** ending should not present much difficulty. The **er** ending must be carefully listened to. It is not quite the same as **er** in the name **Er**nest. However, once the student tackles real words the sound will be entirely familiar.

The grid has been divided into four columns. The first column, in the shaded area, has examples of the rules for syllable division. The new rule is:

Never divide: ing.

The second column contains polynons which must be divided with a pencil and earn a tick when they have been divided correctly.

Dots and dates are not needed.

Columns three and four contain polynons which your student must read. Two ticks are needed on separate occasions. Once again, dots and dates are not needed.

All the other rules for syllable division must be observed.

Examples	Divide only	Read only		Read only	
rinn/ock/er	topnitter	flexipode		nathommer	
un/dimm/er	aplogging	itchapper		sandanker	
teff/ann/ing	teffender	slaftons		hassondip	
itch/add/er	fogapting	japstander		stromding	
mif/tax/er	grintanding	indrabbing		thiptatter	
fress/ing	chatrimming	thrensade		etchipping	
lott/ash/ing	indripping	oxidropper		saggondap	
len/dagg/er	brinsilfer	slickasling		iglatcher	
ill/senn/er	cutrummer	sapponder		frondammer	
ock/att/ing	paxamander	twimmoffat		sliggonther	
atch/onn/er	ickelting	thrumming		crumfatter	
biff/ath/ing	skimmoning	grittamanx		jobbanning	

Other Information

Real Words

Coach

Make sure your student knows that these are real words.

Each pair of words needs to earn three consecutive ticks.

Each tick must be earned on a different day.

Tick the positives and dot the negatives.

Make sure you work on any negatives before you leave the page.

	Day											Day								
	Month											Month								
better	runner									stiffer	ladder									
clapper	rubber									hiccup	letter									
stopper	dropping									glitter	butter									
stunner	flatter									slimming	fitter									
brimming	gritter									sniffing	flutter									
scatter	supper									slipping	slipper									
traffic	bigger									horrid	stutter									
sinner	tripper									copper	digging									
clatter	cladding									dapper	jogging									
sadder	matter									grinning	jamming									
dripping	trotting									fatter	bidding									
many	house									people	call									

Other Information

Sentences

Coach

Ask the student to read the sentences. If all the words are read correctly tick the box.

1. Underline any words in a sentence which have not been read correctly and coach them.

2. After a period of **not less** than twenty-four hours you must ask the student to attempt the underlined words once more. When the student knows the word put a bar **(/)** through the underline with a pencil.

3. Tick the box when all the underlined words in a sentence have been barred. Dates are not required. However, you must keep returning to the underlined words until all boxes have been ticked.

The full sentence needs to be read once only but the underlined words must then be coached.

Never bar a word on the day that you coach it.

People who don't bother to find time to help each other are often sad.

Call at the kitchen before all the children go to the house for dinner.

Spring is a better time to plant the cuttings in a garden or an allotment.

The butter on the girl's platter was for the faster of the diggers.

In the house you will find Monica's mother, brother and five sisters.

Picking and pecking is not the way to have dinner with a chum.

Many people call the other number to upset the new club members.

"Walk on the path and not on the tramway," said Emma to her sister.

The sender of the cutting was doing the shopping for his mother.

The kippers in the cabinet were given to the hungry cat.

The butler is rubbing the silver and his hands are getting hotter.

Don't call for me if you cannot find a hammer to strike the rusty peg.

Sing for your supper and your children can have some fish and chips.

Many people came and went but others never came at all.

Walk with your mother and call at their home but don't go inside.

Other Information

The two sounds of 'oo'

Toe by Toe's usual method is to make the student read polynons and then real words. However, with 'oo' we are faced with a choice of sounds and this can cause problems for students with reading difficulties. It is better that students make their choice from the structure of real words.

Coach

Make sure your student knows that these are real words. This exercise introduces the two sounds of **oo**. Listen to the sound made by the **oo** as in m**oo**n and **oo** as in g**oo**d. Familiarise your student with both these sounds before you start.

Most mistakes will result from the student applying the wrong sound of **oo** to the word. A simple substitution of one sound of **oo** for the other will usually suffice. In such cases a word earns a dot.

Both words in a pair must be read correctly to earn a tick.

Each pair needs to earn three consecutive ticks.

Each tick must be earned on a different day (not less than twenty-four hours).

		Day							
		Month							
food	croon								
boom	moose								
fooling	root								
shooting	loot								
spoon	shoot								
looping	swoon								
trooper	droopy								
grooming	brooding								
blooming	stool								
roof	mood								
boot	doom								
were	now								

		Day							
		Month							
cooking	good								
content	blood								
flooding	shook								
thinking	stood								
booking	selfish								
rook	manhood								
looking	soot								
cook	varnish								
complex	crook								
brook	confide								
foot	took								
how	down								

Other Information

Sentences

With the introduction of a few more Link Words and new skills the sentences are becoming a little more inspiring. However, we must still balance the need for students to build words against a context which allows them to give an inspired guess.

If all the words in the English language could be categorised into groups of strictly delineated phonic patterns our task would be a great deal easier. In some cases, where the sound of a word does not exactly match the skill required to read it, we use both the context and the student's word building skills to advance their general reading ability.

Coach

Ask the student to read the sentences. If all the words are read correctly tick the box.

1. Underline any words in a sentence which have not been read correctly and coach them.

2. After a period of **not less** than twenty-four hours you must ask the student to attempt the underlined words once more. When the student knows the word put a bar **(/)** through the underline with a pencil.

3. Tick the box when all the underlined words in a sentence have been barred. Dates are not required. However, you must keep returning to the underlined words until all boxes have been ticked.

The full sentence needs to be read once only but the underlined words must then be coached.

Never bar a word on the day that you coach it.

Shall we go now or shall we take a walk when the sun goes down?

"How can I mend these nets?" said the skipper of the fishing vessel.

How did the other gardener shake the buds to make them droop?

Now is not the time to brood over the floods in the West.

"If you were not so tall you could fit in the van," said the driver.

Take the wooden plate, a sharp blade, a silver spoon and a goblet.

Swoop on the crooks and tell the cooks how to bake a cake.

Tell the fool that it is rude to look down on other people.

Choose good tools to loosen the nuts and bolts on the car.

It is very cool by the brook so put on your woollen hood and scarf.

Put the loose loop over the foot of the rook and let it fly to the roof.

The cook and I were in the kitchen when the stove began to smoke.

Give Micky and Jim more time to fill the groove with smoother wood.

Many people can use the tools to give the wood a smoother finish.

Go now and put the noose on the goose and don't let it loose.

Other Information

Revision

We cannot stress too often the importance of revision exercises. Skills learned in earlier exercises must be dragged back into focus until they operate at a subliminal level.

The note concerning the hard sound of the letter 's' could have been introduced earlier but we have found that it is preferable to omit as many rules as possible in the earlier stages. At this stage of the book, students seem to be more receptive to the range of words that a simple rule can operate.

Doors are beginning to open.

Coach

This is a revision exercise.

Make sure your student knows that these are real words.

Each pair of words needs to earn three consecutive ticks.

Each tick must be earned on a different day.

Tick the positives and dot the negatives.

Make sure you work on any negatives before you leave the page.

Note: The letter **s** sometimes adopts the sound of the letter **z** as in the word: **rise**. The sense of the word will help your student make the choice.

		Day									
		Month									
choose	pools										
trooper	packing										
thunder	scandal										
looms	gone										
looting	attack										
stood	thing										
thicken	spender										
hooting	use										
backing	mood										
goes	chicken										
thicker	wool										
would	both										

		Day									
		Month									
ratchet	rose										
hooter	match										
thorn	pose										
hatchet	stuck										
aloof	trick										
jacket	deck										
sack	booking										
want	thinner										
loot	hooks										
stitch	groom										
rise	pluck										
open	because										

Check any previously completed grids for words which have not earned three ticks in a row.

Other Information

Polynons using 'ee'

Coach

Point out that the twin vowels **ee** can make only one sound: **ee** as in **tree**. Double **ee** *always* says **ee** as in **tree**.

Ask the student to read the polynons on the opposite page. When a polynon has been read correctly you must tick the first box. Dates are not required.

The other box can be ticked when the polynon has been read correctly on another occasion. Dots are not needed.

If your student has difficulty, ask him/her to read the polynon syllable by syllable, using the skills developed in the syllable division exercises.

Ask your student to divide them in his/her head. A pencil should not be used.

Read only		**Read only**		**Read only**		**Read only**	
cheeming		reenisher		teelapode		chentipper	
ackeemode		threebing		atcheemop		crasticker	
slebsobby		bletteemer		robbatrack		slottopeen	
moppeensip		skeltaply		deeshome		reetacker	
optimees		grimdaston		checkateem		slickeep	
agtestofe		grassinsot		beebaxing		rappotting	
swisteeper		reeltimper		trickaleen		gleeting	
snefradly		sleetode		maldeeber		threetiffope	
spostenly		sheemer		creevaxer		respicking	
undaffog		steening		switcherteef		shaftipe	
meediflan		gleenadly		veemoller		isherdock	
cleggondag		creefode		dreekash		otchapash	
domseetand		senpeeter		apixeeding		leedanker	

Other Information

Real Words

As the letters **'ee'** make the one uncomplicated sound we can expect a student to read the words in this exercise without too much difficulty.

It is time to stretch their skills. They must now read all four words in a line to earn a tick.

Coach

Make sure your student knows that these are real words.

All four words in a line must be read correctly to earn a tick.

Each line needs to earn three consecutive ticks.

Each tick must be earned on a different day (not less than twenty-four hours).

The Link Word **where** is often confused with **were**. Should this confusion occur; use the following memory aid (mnemonic):

Where is the chair?

The lower case **h** in the word w**h**ere can be likened to the profile of a dining room chair. The rhyme helps the student to remember that the **h** belongs in the word **where** and not **were**.

| | Day |
| | Month |

bleed feeds weed creeping

creed creel reef fleeting

steel sheer seep freezing

weeps geese meet peeling

greet Greek flee meeting

sheep cheer Tees steeper

needs cheek peer agreement

sheen sleek keen freedom

creep Leeds beer creeper

preen seen heed disagree

deeds feet glee disagreement

old where there give

Other Information

Sentences

Coach

Ask the student to read the sentences. If all the words are read correctly tick the box.

1. Underline any words in a sentence which have not been read correctly and coach them.

2. After a period of **not less** than twenty-four hours you must ask the student to attempt the underlined words once more. When the student knows the word put a bar **(/)** through the underline with a pencil.

3. Tick the box when all the underlined words in a sentence have been barred. Dates are not required. However, you must keep returning to the underlined words until all boxes have been ticked.

The full sentence needs to be read once only but the underlined words must then be coached.

This exercise covers three pages.

Never bar a word on the day that you coach it.

Where is the old man who took shelter in the park on Sunday?

"I was born in a small house in the street over there," said Martin.

Did you feed the three creeping geese that were seen on the Green?

If I were you I would give the Greek people a ride on the green bus.

The gates to both houses were open because the milkman had been.

"Give me your hands," said the woman to both of her children.

"Have you seen the bees on the chestnut tree?" said Jane.

"Greet the others and feed the sheep in the steep creek," said Bob.

The sweet girl was sitting over there in the shade of the beech tree.

Is this where the sheep on the steep street had freezing feet?

If the people sniff pepper on the breeze it will make them sneeze.

Weeding the big open garden will give old Jack a stiff back.

The breeze was from the North because it froze the sheets on the line.

Fifteen cheering girls would often drink hot milk in the streets of Leeds.

Sleep is often difficult for both teething children and their mums.

Have you been to the steep creek where the trees make you itch?

Where can we find a shop that sells boots, handbags and slippers?

Is this where the farmer gives the feed to her greedy sheep?

"Shall I see if the bride is late?" said the groom to the best man.

"Could you slide down the creeper?" said Tarzan to the chimp.

Send for the seed cake and tell them to fetch it on the old green tray.

If you pay heed to your speed when driving in the mist you will be safe.

Where were you when the others were playing hide and seek?

Some lamps would be lit in the street but not in the morning.

The mariner felt confident that he could steer the large hovercraft.

The banker would not play with his green kite because it was too wet.

We have an agreement because it gives us the freedom to march.

"In the dale you will find the open car with the black hood," said Mandy.

"Greetings!" said Lee. "It is good to see you looking so well."

"Good teeth make smiles seem more cheerful," said the dentist.

Both of the old fisherman's nets were full of eels and pike.

Is it too late to give Janet her birthday present before she goes home?

"Let's go to the match," said Molly to Anna. "We can get the tickets now."

How will both sheep feed on the small patch of green grass over there?

If you want the bus for London you must go down to the end of the lane.

The girls may call at the butcher's shop after they have been to the match.

If she would do all the things that she should we could all go home.

Metal shutters may protect the shopkeeper's premises from vandals.

Shall I call or will you go and see if the shop will open before lunch?

The level of input was not up to standard said the man from the Ministry.

Seemingly, the girl has decreed that the grass must be free from weeds.

We must establish good standards in both agriculture and industry.

She was seething with anger because Sheena always disagreed with Lee.

We could not sleep because we ate a late dinner of beef and cheese.

Compile the report, walk to the docks, then take a ship to Norway.

Other Information

Real words introducing two sounds of 'ea'

'ea' like 'oo' presents confusion if it is couched in a polynon and likewise the exceptions: steak, break, beauty…etc.

Coach

Remind your student that these are real words.

Generally the letters **ea** make two sounds: **ea** as in **tea** and **ea** as in **head**. Familiarise him/her with both sounds.

The choice of sound should be made mentally before a verbal commitment is made. Do not allow him/her to chop and change. The first answer counts.

Both words in a pair must be read correctly to earn a tick.

Each pair needs to earn three consecutive ticks.

Each tick must be earned on a different day (not less than twenty-four hours).

	Day													Day										
	Month													Month										
pleasant	reaching											leash	stealing										
beads	tea											jeans	dealer										
leaks	beans											clean	healing										
stealth	grease											neater	cleaner										
health	pleat											weaker	heather										
weaker	stream											heater	please										
dealt	beaker											peasant	weather										
pleading	cheaper											wealth	speaker										
cheater	dread											wealthy	teams										
beams	peach											tease	feather										
feast	heat											cream	beach										
bleat	leather											leaves	heaping										
saw	another											woman	know										

Other Information

Sentences

Coach

Ask the student to read the sentences. If all the words are read correctly tick the box.

1. Underline any words in a sentence which have not been read correctly and coach them.

2. After a period of **not less** than twenty-four hours you must ask the student to attempt the underlined words once more. When the student knows the word put a bar (/) through the underline with a pencil.

3. Tick the box when all the underlined words in a sentence have been barred. Dates are not required. However, you must keep returning to the underlined words until all boxes have been ticked.

The full sentence needs to be read once only but the underlined words must then be coached.

This exercise covers three pages.

Never bar a word on the day that you coach it.

Do you know the woman who came to the park with her children?

The woman took her dog for a walk on the pleasant heathland.

A freak and unpleasant wind made us shiver and shake.

The bird saw the bread and cheese on the plate but it did not eat it.

The greedy deer ate the weeds and another deer ate the heather.

The reason Mr Green was cheating could be clearly seen.

I fear the beer will not clear in time for the feast at Easter.

The lean meat eater had a belt made of bone and leather.

Please take heed and do not tread on the green carpet.

Put all the old grease in the tub and the fresh cream on the plate.

"Head for home!" said the leader of the beaten cricket team.

The cleaner dreads eating jam and bread because it makes him fat.

Another woman came to the last match and saw the team win.

Did you know the mean cheater who made his wealth by stealth?

The peasant was unpleasant because he had eaten some bitter leaves.

Come with me to the store and get some bread and cheese for your tea.

"Can I go to another match?" said the girl to her mother.

Beat the eggs for fifteen seconds and then add the cream and cheese.

If you like good food you may dream of eating green beans for tea.

Spread the bread with butter and eat plenty of meat.

Do you know the tall woman who has left her shopping on the shelf?

Most of the beech tree's leaves fell in the month of November.

Wipe the sweat from your head and put on a clean sweatband.

If you sleep in the barn the feathers and grass may stick to your jeans.

The speaker was pleading for the teachers to eat some of the peaches.

The healthy farmer could leap over the sheep, the pigs and the geese.

"Eat the bread and leave the meat in the oven," said the baker.

The cook had to deal with the old grease which was left on the freezer.

The mattress was made of leather and plastic because duck and goose feathers make some people sneeze.

The woman did not know that her old hat was made from feathers.

I fear the mud has made the stream dirty and unfit to drink.

The heap of stones was too heavy for his mother to carry.

If you ate black bread for your tea you may eat another cream bun.

"Thread the cotton and mend my dress quickly," said the rude customer.

Neglect can soon make the landscape look dreary and dismal.

The head of the class will lead the people from the West.

"Is there a reason for all this unseasonal activity?" said the woman.

The creaking gate made sleep difficult for the old man.

"Reach out and grab the leather loop," said the driver of the bus.

"Please put a penny in the old man's hat," said the carol singer.

The feathers in her hat came from the head of the peacock.

Please reap the corn and thresh it in the yard by the barn.

Readers in the departmental reading room would not speak to the new assistant because she was always unpleasant and very unhelpful.

Other Information

Polynons, introducing the vowel combination: 'oa'

Coach

In the vowel combination **oa** the first vowel takes the long sound: in this case **o**. listen to the sound of **oa** in **boat**. Ask the student to ignore the **a** and give the **o** its long sound. It should not take long for them to get the idea.

Ask the student to read the polynons on the opposite page. When a polynon has been read correctly you must tick the first box. Dates and dots are not needed. The other box can be ticked when the polynon has been read correctly on another occasion.

If your student has difficulty, ask him/her to read the polynon syllable by syllable, using the skills developed in the syllable division exercises.

Syllable division should be carried out mentally (no pencils). If this causes anxiety, a piece of card moved along the polynon, stopping at the divisions will help.

Do not forget that this is a reading exercise.

Note: Ticks are given for *reading* a polynon and not for dividing it.

Read

teemanoat

flickoading

radpoadate

poyrickoag

poamancher

sayroaper

sipaytoan

poatachip

shandoach

soalatch

thoatrack

estoaming

pithoasher

Read

stoapack

spoamife

leftoapoy

moyoach

bentoamarp

spoacher

toathank

froamend

shoathick

tatchoak

groamasp

oapanick

groashank

Read

reetoad

drammoat

roaftank

loapine

droadap

ackoanip

oastipper

inganoap

poadrattop

toashaft

grimmoacher

skilnoad

droabing

Read

itchimoan

astoafing

cloapish

ratternoach

snoamafting

bloachoth

drichoap

shoafape

pathoag

littoan

hickoash

troamack

otchanoaf

Other Information

Real Words

In this exercise we have mixed **Link Words** amongst words containing the **'oa'** combination in order to discourage students from merely pre-empting the answers.

	Day												Day										
	Month												Month										
coat	why											boat	coal										
many	goal											coast	poach										
when	loan											boating	foam										
people	you											roast	throat										
now	float											toast	they										
gone	foal											are	soap										
soak	shoal											moat	your										
too	toaster											goat	over										
road	load											were	poacher										
groan	moan											any	boast										
coach	toad											Joan	stoat										
couldn't through												water	above										

Other Information

Sentences

Coach

Ask the student to read the sentences. If all the words are read correctly tick the box.

1. Underline any words in a sentence which have not been read correctly and coach them.

2. After a period of **not less** than twenty-four hours you must ask the student to attempt the underlined words once more. When the student knows the word put a bar (/) through the underline with a pencil.

3. Tick the box when all the underlined words in a sentence have been barred. Dates are not required. However, you must keep returning to the underlined words until all boxes have been ticked.

The full sentence needs to be read once only but the underlined words must then be coached.

Never bar a word on the day that you coach it.

People drink water from the stream by the lake because it is clear.

"Above all!", said Martha, "do not go down to the end of the road."

"Don't hang your coat on the rusty hook," said Joan.

The woman in the black coat asked for a loan to buy a new car.

The cook couldn't toast the thick bread in the new toaster.

He couldn't think of a reason to stay so he went home and read a book.

Above the road the groaning wind could be heard in the wires.

Take the coach through the dock gates and cross the sea to Norway.

Roast some chestnuts over the coal fire and keep watching the stove.

A good festival in times of adversity is a splendid way to end the day.

When and where can I catch the next boat to New Zealand?

You should not approach the man on the coach if he wears a black hat.

The referee told the players not to stand in front of the goal.

Shoals of fish eat loads of food as they swim through the deep water.

The man carrying the sack of coal couldn't open the heavy gate.

Other Information

Polynons containing the vowel combination 'ai'

Coach

As with the vowel combination **oa** the letters **ai** act in the same way: **the first letter takes the long sound and the last letter is silent**. 'ai' says **ai** as in tr**ai**n. Ask the student to forget the **i** and say the long sound of the **a**.

Ask the student to **read** the polynons on the opposite page. When a polynon has been read correctly you must tick the first box. Dates and dots are not needed. The other box can be ticked when the polynon has been read correctly on another occasion.

If your student has difficulty, ask him/her to read the polynon, syllable by syllable, using the skills developed in the syllable division exercises.

Syllable division should be carried out mentally (no pencils). If this causes anxiety, a piece of card moved along the polynon, stopping at the divisions, will help but **do not forget that this is a reading exercise.**

Read

maipattoy

baitish

raidpate

ainpecker

painaytog

ensaikrip

aidappot

clenfoach

taiterpoy

naindope

logaiding

topaining

mondailer

loytailer

Read

claifing

taishine

troysait

megpaith

camtain

stepsimail

sockibain

crimpain

aintigger

pitchaiting

ackainpate

blendaif

stainatch

gaisathoy

Read

skataik

raskail

traimoath

thaindrap

slaikath

plaimink

snaicher

laibatting

traifindop

drailannop

oachaider

collainite

ailstipper

laidommint

Read

praiminitch

paidinker

laideetoaf

teenoach

chinpail

toadain

broachain

aibandeck

chamfait

intaspofe

itchaimer

dipaimine

critchaid

naidanker

Other Information

Real Words

Link Words interrupt the pattern of sound expectation which often arises when we deal with words which contain a dominant vowel combination such as **'ai'**.

Coach

Make sure your student knows that these are real words.

Each pair of words needs to earn three consecutive ticks.

Each tick must be earned on a different day.

Tick the positives and dot the negatives.

Make sure you work on any negatives before you leave the page.

	Day											Day									
	Month											Month									
mail	railing										claim	other									
gone	should										raider	call									
drain	who										trail	done									
maid	trains										open	chains									
most	does										why	plain									
one	all										painter	brain									
gain	grain										your	contain									
could	railway										both	sailing									
where	woman										trainer	they									
remain	tail										here	disdain									
what	because										would	failing									
asked	enough										only	idea									

Other Information

Sentences

Coach

Ask the student to read the sentences. If all the words are read correctly tick the box.

1. Underline any words in a sentence which have not been read correctly and coach them.

2. After a period of **not less** than twenty-four hours you must ask the student to attempt the underlined words once more. When the student knows the word put a bar **(/)** through the underline with a pencil.

3. Tick the box when all the underlined words in a sentence have been barred. Dates are not required. However, you must keep returning to the underlined words until all boxes have been ticked.

The full sentence needs to be read once only but the underlined words must then be coached.

The words are longer and more complicated. If your student doesn't read the word correctly ask him/her to make a simple switch of vowel sounds from long to short or vice-versa. Usually, this is all that is needed to read the word correctly.

Never bar a word on the day that you coach it.

These clothes are only good enough to wear for digging the garden.

"Have you had enough to eat?" the waitress asked pleasantly.

Only the trainer could train the seals to clap their flippers.

The woman claims that she was made to wait for the train in the rain.

Rain and hail have made the path very unpleasant for the old men.

Both kings and peasants feel pain and strain when they are ill.

A man from Spain made bread from grain and asked the boy to eat it.

A Greek man had an idea in the bath and ran off before he was dry.

The prisoner was told that he could only have bail if he was good.

It is a good idea to maintain your drains and keep them clean.

Meat alone is not enough to sustain those who need plenty of bread.

Some foods contain far too much fat to maintain a healthy life.

The mainmast broke and the ship was lost in the mist and rain.

Mr Braidy asked if the train standing on the platform was from Bath.

Other Information

Revision of Link Words

Link Words must be consolidated. Sentences alone may not guarantee enough instances of these words to establish them as part of a student's vocabulary.

Coach

This is an important exercise. Revision is vital. We need to consolidate the student's skills.

Make sure your student knows that these are real words.

Each pair of words needs to earn three consecutive ticks.

Each tick must be earned on a different day.

Tick the positives and dot the negatives.

Make sure you work on any negatives before you leave the page.

Coach negatives as you would any Link Word. Repeat them over and over again.

		Day										
		Month										
what	you											
here	her											
who	their											
why	does											
each	girl											
use	before											
came	some											
have	want											
these	small											
new	tall											
your	said											
walk	don't											

		Day										
		Month										
are	find											
gone	they											
most	woman											
would	many											
both	other											
open	people											
because	call											
old	were											
where	knew											
there	how											
give	down											
could	through											

Other Information

'ed' at the end of a word

Most people never consider the choice of sounds incumbent upon these letters or the problems they cause people with reading difficulties. Once again we could introduce a complicated set of rules. For example: **'ed'** after **'ch'** always makes a **'t'** sound.

Why burden the coach and pupil? Real words cannot be read correctly with an inappropriate **'ed'** ending. The word itself determines the choice.

Coach

The letters **ed** at the end of a word make one of three sounds. Listen to the sound made by the **bold** letters in the following words.

pushed   united   planned

You will notice that the word **pushed** sounds as if it ends with the letter **t**.

The second word has a strange ending. The sound begins with a short hardly stressed grunt which falls between the short sounds of **e** and **u** and ends with the short sound of **d**.

The third word sounds as if it should be spelled:

pland

Listen carefully to the sounds made by the examples. The word **pushed** like the word **reached** can only adopt one sound. The student will select the ending which follows naturally.

Words sharing the same ending have been paired.

The three tick rule applies.

	Day									
	Month									
toasted	fainted									
pressed	clipped									
claimed	drained									
lifted	sifted									
chopped	dropped									
streamed	cleaned									
painted	mended									
dipped	shipped									
trailed	failed									
sorted	floated									
chipped	nipped									
planted	granted									
none	which									

	Day									
	Month									
patched	matched									
sailed	wailed									
admitted	fitted									
tripped	gripped									
planned	manned									
landed	branded									
sacked	backed									
moaned	groaned									
healed	sealed									
stepped	tipped									
creamed	beamed									
slapped	clapped									
pretty	told									

Other Information

Sentences

Coach

Ask the student to read the sentences. If all the words are read correctly tick the box.

1. Underline any words in a sentence which have not been read correctly and coach them.

2. After a period of **not less** than twenty-four hours you must ask the student to attempt the underlined words once more. When the student knows the word put a bar (/) through the underline with a pencil.

3. Tick the box when all the underlined words in a sentence have been barred. Dates are not required. However, you must keep returning to the underlined words until all boxes have been ticked.

The full sentence needs to be read once only but the underlined words must then be coached.

Never bar a word on the day that you coach it.

"None of my orders were understood", barked the angry admiral.

The sentimentalist said, "Everything was so pretty in those days."

A realist told the sentimentalist that those days were pretty bad.

If only the woman had told me she was tired I could have helped her.

He wined and dined and passed the port until it was time to go.

He tripped over the basket of bleached clothes and landed on his back.

After some time it was clear that none of the girls would arrive.

Only the bearded man attended the meeting in a tailored jacket.

She pegged the tattered sheet on the line and dined on grilled ham.

The man in the tinted glasses liked roasted nuts and creamed broccoli.

He would only eat the oysters which were served with buttered toast.

The hooded man robbed the bank and dropped the cash as he ran.

Irene dreaded the exam because she had neglected to read her notes.

Which way did the fast boat go and who was splashed by the waves?

The paint on the board was flaked and blistered by the hot sun.

Other Information

Losing the Mute 'e'

It would not be difficult to totally confuse the student by giving them rules about tense changes or by telling them that two vowels separated by one consonant will generally give the first vowel the long sound.

We have found that grouping words of the same root has been a much more effective way of teaching students to read these words.

Coach

The mute **e** sometimes operates when we can't see it. Look at the examples below.

skate / skating

We call the word **skate** the **root word** and all the other words such as: **skater skates skating** and **skated** stem from it. If we add the suffixes **ed er ing** and **en** or the plural **s,** the mute **e** will still operate even though it may not actually be visible.

All three words need to be read correctly to earn a tick.

Make sure your student knows that these are real words.

Each row needs to earn three consecutive ticks.

Each tick must be earned on a different day.

Tick the positives and dot the negatives.

Make sure you work on any negatives before you leave the page.

			Day										Day						
			Month										Month						
skate	skater	skating							trade	traded	trading								
state	stated	stating							dive	diver	diving								
slope	sloped	sloping							dine	dined	dining								
frame	framed	framing							pine	pined	pining								
file	filed	filing							wipe	wiped	wiping								
bake	baked	baking							pipe	piper	piping								
take	takes	taking							fade	faded	fading								
drive	driver	driving							flame	flamed	flaming								
make	maker	making							hide	hides	hiding								
flake	flaked	flaking							ride	rider	riding								
choke	choked	choking							doze	dozed	dozing								
time	timer	timing							slide	slides	sliding								

Other Information

Revision

Coach

Ask the student to read the sentences. If all the words are read correctly tick the box.

1. Underline any words in a sentence which have not been read correctly and coach them.

2. After a period of **not less** than twenty-four hours you must ask the student to attempt the underlined words once more. When the student knows the word put a bar (/) through the underline with a pencil.

3. Tick the box when all the underlined words in a sentence have been barred. Dates are not required. However, you must keep returning to the underlined words until all boxes have been ticked.

The full sentence needs to be read once only but the underlined words must then be coached.

Never bar a word on the day that you coach it.

By the time the transporter reached the docks the boat was sailing off the French coast which meant that the goods were too late for the sale.

The railings which ran along the side of the railway embankment were rotten making it unsafe for the old people and children living nearby.

The 'Greasy Spoon' snack bar had to close because a cockroach had made its way into the health inspector's ham and mustard sandwich.

"Remember to look after the toast", said Veronica, "and the marmalade is in the pantry next to the broad beans which are under the top shelf."

Taking one's time over dinner is an art which seems to have escaped flesh eating beasts such as the jackal and the grizzly bear.

Having failed to stop his mother from going to Wetherby on the morning train, James felt inclined to eat as many of her chocolates as he could.

The train now standing on platform three is the six thirty express to Bradford calling at Bedford, Doncaster, Leeds and Bradford.

Check any previously completed grids for words which have not earned three ticks in a row.

Other Information

Vowels followed by the letter 'r'

Coach

Read the following list and familiarise your student with the sounds made by the bold letters in the following list of words:

bi**r**d   p**e**r**m   c**u**r**d   sk**i**r**t   f**i**r**m

Tell your student that these vowels followed by the letter **r** usually say **ir** as in b**ir**d and then ask him/her to read the polynons opposite. When a polynon has been read correctly you must tick the first box. Dates and dots are not required. The other box can be ticked when the polynon has been read correctly on another occasion.

If your student has difficulty, ask him/her to read the polynon syllable by syllable, using the skills developed in the syllable division exercises. Syllable division should be carried out mentally (no pencils). If this causes anxiety, a piece of card moved along the polynon, stopping at the divisions, will help but **do not forget that this is a reading exercise.**

Read

purtoash
braipiring
lethirpurl
steelirfint
dreebirn
derpething
spitchnurf
lagsoatirn
leemerpet
cheggirfing
fursoapert
swirpurmer
potchirleen

Read

floamurr
sturlettoap
roagurping
drellirterp
clurfoal
glerfash
wendirper
craipursh
stailirper
cheelerpath
twirlashing
lainersher
lerfatcher

Read

fransirmer
itchirrath
flerith
lasteenerop
spondirlap
laitsiraip
stompering
cleftirish
platterand
flaxerim
cramlotter
raimisteen
coaturfat

Read

plurmitch
brittermat
oxirdoke
itchurtoke
snirring
pollirwisk
goamer
erniloak
furloat
praiternock
spirdask
shirpone
churfing

Other Information

Real Words

Toe by Toe cannot legislate for every nuance of pronunciation. In order to avoid unnecessary pedantry, we allow the student to use word building to construct an approximate sound from which to make an educated attempt.

The word 'thermal' in the first column and 'sherbet' in the second column contain unstressed vowels but it shouldn't take too much prompting for the word to be read correctly.

Coach

Make sure your student knows that these are real words.

Each pair of words needs to earn three consecutive ticks.

Each tick must be earned on a different day.

Tick the positives and dot the negatives.

Make sure you work on any negatives before you leave the page.

Don't forget! We can afford to be generous with some polynon exercises but real words must be read correctly.

	Day												Day								
	Month												Month								
burned	herd											surfing	skirmish								
curling	lurch											turner	person								
churned	burger											dirt	spurt								
firm	Turkish											skirted	mermaid								
burden	curler											chirp	blurred								
Bertha	blur											terminate	purlin								
swirling	currents											third	stirred								
flirted	stern											Burma	murder								
thermal	hurting											birch	furnished								
lurking	unfurl											hurled	sherbet								
servant	spurned											thirsty	disturb								
twirl	twirling											dirty	curt								
one	someone											without	anyone								

Other Information

Sentences

Coach

Ask the student to read the sentences. If all the words are read correctly tick the box.

1. Underline any words in a sentence which have not been read correctly and coach them.

2. After a period of **not less** than twenty-four hours you must ask the student to attempt the underlined words once more. When the student knows the word put a bar **(/)** through the underline with a pencil.

3. Tick the box when all the underlined words in a sentence have been barred. Dates are not required. However, you must keep returning to the underlined words until all boxes have been ticked.

The full sentence needs to be read once only but the underlined words must then be coached.

Never bar a word on the day that you coach it.

The old farmer left one of the rusty churns by the churchyard gate and returned to the farm with a crate on the back of his dirty old truck.

"Consider this", said Mr Merton, "some things are much easier to read than others and without the facts none of this is relevant to anyone."

"Ask yourself this," said Bert, "if someone was hurt in a skirmish with the enemy on Thursday, would they be taken prisoner or sent to the infirmary?"

The man asked the waiter if anyone could tell him the correct way to cook lobster thermidor and turkey without getting his hands dirty or greasy.

Someone solved the murder mystery but was it Agatha or was it Sherlock who took the credit for it?

The pretty girl unfurled the flag and then stood on the leather chair because the feather duster was forever making her nose twitch.

Everything was still and one of the old Kurdish women slept, curled up, on the fur coats on the third bed further along the corridor.

Other Information

Words containing the vowel combinations 'ar' & 'or'

We have already mentioned that we need one common rule to deal with words containing **vowel / r** combinations. We are aware of the complications. The sound **'or'** in the word 'w**or**k' and **'or'** in the word fact**or**y are different.

Matters can be complicated even further by regional pronunciations. To ask students with reading problems not to stress certain vowels or to put an inflexion in some cases and not in others is a recipe for distress. It is enough for them to understand a common rule for all and build a word which approximates to the one they are attempting to read.

When a choice of sounds exists, polynons can prove to be awkward to read and now that we have added the combinations **'ar'**, **'or'**, and **'our'**, real words will be of more use to the student.

Coach

Ask your student to listen to the sound made by the **bold** letters at the end of the following words.

coll**ar**   pol**ar**   tract**or**   col**our**

An exact sound is hard to define. However, if your student thinks of the sound of **ir** as in b**ir**d, it will not take him/her long to find the correct sound.

Make sure your student knows that these are real words.

Each pair of words needs to earn three consecutive ticks.

Each tick must be earned on a different day.

Tick the positives and dot the negatives.

Make sure you work on any negatives before you leave the page.

	Day									Day								
	Month									Month								

Note! The letters **or** / **ar** / **our** in the words: tract**or**, coll**ar** and flav**our** make the same sound.

vector	detector							visitor	someone						
rector	work							error	anybody						
selector	firework							burglar	nobody						
doctor	working							grammar	forever						
sailor	worm							collector	however						
harbour	vigour							rigour	colour						
Hector	word							sector	yourself						
terror	worst							collar	himself						
factor	candour							pillar	whatever						
victor	monitor							dollar	endless						
beggar	senator							vendor	inside						
actor	pastor							tractor	undergo						
inspect	factory							protector	overturn						
talk	laugh							friend	move						

Other Information

Sentences

Coach

Ask the student to read the sentences. If all the words are read correctly tick the box.

1. Underline any words in a sentence which have not been read correctly and coach them.

2. After a period of **not less** than twenty-four hours you must ask the student to attempt the underlined words once more. When the student knows the word put a bar **(/)** through the underline with a pencil.

3. Tick the box when all the underlined words in a sentence have been barred. Dates are not required. However, you must keep returning to the underlined words until all boxes have been ticked.

The full sentence needs to be read once only but the underlined words must then be coached.

Never bar a word on the day that you coach it.

Bertram, the bearded, bungling burglar from Bury, broke into the prison and stole a mailbag, only to find that he couldn't escape because his tunnel was blocked.

"Don't blame the girl in the fur coat, " interrupted the inspector, "she was only standing next to the murdered man. Her friend is the person I need to talk to most of all."

You cannot put a collar on the driver of the tractor because someone in the sector is using a metal detector in an attempt to find the person who laughed as he waved a dirty feather duster which he stole from a department store in Birmingham.

Valour, honour and fair play are not easily recognised traits in the demeanour of some of the birds and animals which roam or fly over the African plains.

Consider your move with care and you had better not talk to his friend because he too plays chess every day and any move you make could reach his ears.

The vicar and the rector could not agree to marry people who wanted to scatter lots of confetti over the churchyard on Saturday afternoon.

The burly contractor took the big tractor, the bulldozer and the dumper, so that he could demolish the factory in time for tea and then laugh all the way to the bank.

The dentist from Wolverhampton spoke at some length and with candour on the very painful subject of clinical orthodontics as practised in children's hospitals.

Other Information

More Sentences/Passages

As the number of word building skills increases we can start to make our sentences longer, more complex and more interesting. Students will find these sentences and short passages an enjoyable challenge.

Coach

This exercise is the same as the previous exercise but the sentences are longer.

Ask the student to read the sentences / passages. If all the words are read correctly tick the box.

1. Underline any words in a sentence which have not been read correctly and coach them.

2. After a period of **not less** than twenty-four hours you must ask the student to attempt the underlined words once more. When the student knows the word put a bar **(/)** through the underline with a pencil.

3. Tick the box when all the underlined words in a sentence have been barred. Dates are not required. However, you must keep returning to the underlined words until all boxes have been ticked.

The full sentence needs to be read once only but the underlined words must then be coached.

Never bar a word on the day that you coach it.

He trained in the rain for the main event. He remembered the words of the absurd coach who had said, "I think it is better to train in all weathers." He was working very hard and was short of breath but he was hoping to win honour and nothing less than a silver medal at the forthcoming Olympic Games.

The boat was dipping in the heavy swell and the coastline could not be seen. The mate had said that it was going to be a bad day to sail but if anybody had agreed with him they had said not a word to the purser who normally took it upon himself to speak for the ship's company in such matters. The deck hands did not bother to complain because they were not due for shore leave anyway.

The copper wire was a good conductor but the electric current was still too strong and the system was soon overloaded. There was a terrific bang as burner after burner exploded. The alarm bell was broken and a fire soon developed amongst the dry wood turnings which covered the workshop floor. A huge pillar of smoke could be seen clearly from the suburbs that were perched on the hills above.

A cabinet leak made the Chancellor angry and led to the rumour that his trusted secretary was no longer 'flavour of the month', with the men from the Ministry of Health.

Other Information

Soft 'g' polynons

Some rules cannot be avoided. However, the rule for soft 'g' is clear and easy to follow.

Coach

We usually think of the sound of the letter **g** making the sound of **g** for **gun** or **girl**. However, this is not always the sound made by the letter **g**. Listen to the sound of the letter in the following sentence.

Gerald went to Germany to agitate the gentle gipsy.

Every **g** in the above sentence makes a sound normally associated with the letter **j**. We call this the 'soft sound' of **g**. This sound usually operates when the **g** is followed by an **i** or an **e**. The rule is: **g** followed by an **i**, **e** or **y** says **'j'** (as in **jam**). There are exceptions to this rule but not for our purposes. In the polynon exercises there are no exceptions.

Ask the student to read the polynons on the opposite page. When a polynon has been read correctly, you must tick the first box. Dates and dots are not required. The other box can be ticked when the polynon has been read correctly on another occasion.

If your student has difficulty, ask him/her to read the polynon, syllable by syllable, using the skills developed in the syllable division exercises. The polynons must be divided mentally (no pencils). If this causes anxiety, a piece of card may be moved along the polynon stopping at each division.

Read		**Read**		**Read**		**Read**	
ropgilter		blofger		margickait		grabgerm	
stergit		geritotch		geratching		rapgerpond	
gendeemer		magistank		agsobgerm		patgerrat	
repgedobe		repgittop		gribbenter		gerasticate	
gennerpoad		gemmerish		gertipode		nitgirabe	
gentickain		argipode		sapginate		gipoader	
lapgend		lefargem		germinock		moolgorf	
gemmigroat		abirnarger		palgatofe		gerushipole	
giplaput		itchimgern		wotgeroam		gimmarank	
furgiment		burgesting		gerkist		swetgirfoam	
sargestain		fargellop		pantergap		cleesipash	
gipgepper		borgibun		fayrapger		timmergip	
elgistaff		stimgerp		tabbergick		gippergun	

Other Information

Words containing the soft 'g' sound

Coach

Unlike the polynon exercises, real words have exceptions to the rule. However, the exceptions are common words and your student will learn them quickly.

Make sure your student knows that these are real words.

Each pair of words needs to earn three consecutive ticks.

Each tick must be earned on a different day.

Tick the positives and dot the negatives.

Make sure you work on any negatives before you leave the page.

		Day											Day							
		Month											Month							
gent	tragic								stages	agile								
gem	genetic								revenge	urgent								
German	Reginald								manager	longer								
energy	barge								germ	gorilla								
forger	Hamburg								plunge	finger								
engage	burger								staged	gender								
raged	magic								gipsy	agenda								
barrage	splurge								digit	Gemma								
dagger	grilled								sponge	rigged								
grease	lethargic								tiger	refuge								
agility	ginger								Gerald	caged								
logical	digger								large	charge								

Other Information

Sentences introducing 'dg'

The combination of the letters 'd' and 'g' is common in many English words. The 'd' makes the reader use the short sound of the preceding vowel.

Coach

This is a normal sentence exercise but we have introduced words like **midget**. When **dg** is found in a word, tell the student to drop the **d** and give the **g** its soft sound. Mark the exercise in the usual way.

Ask the student to read the sentences. If all the words are read correctly tick the box.

1. Underline any words in a sentence which have not been read correctly and coach them.

2. After a period of **not less** than twenty-four hours you must ask the student to attempt the underlined words once more. When the student knows the word put a bar (/) through the underline with a pencil.

3. Tick the box when all the underlined words in a sentence have been barred. Dates are not required. However, you must keep returning to the underlined words until all boxes have been ticked.

The full sentence needs to be read once only but the underlined words must then be coached.

Never bar a word on the day that you coach it.

Mr Rodgers missed the match because he had tripped over a pan of porridge. The absurd logic of the badger baiter's dodgy methods led the judges to fill their ledgers with an assortment of charges against some very unpleasant poachers. "Strange as it may seem, the range of the artist is very limited," said the painter.

The midget was not asked to pass judgement on the state of the juggler's rotten oranges but you could see that the ringmaster was not too happy. It was the acrobat who had first lodged the complaint; having slipped on the peel just before the start of the second act he had hurt his back and was extremely unhappy. His mother screeched and raged at the doctor, "Don't you hurt my Gerald!"

"The woman is mad," snarled the expert, "genetic factors are involved." The old general was not impressed: "I have given you all the time you need to supply the results," he groaned. "If you want magic, I can recommend a witch doctor but I make judgements on facts," returned the expert with venom. "Engage the enemy with fixed bayonets," the general boomed but no one was listening.

Other Information

Soft 'c' polynons

The majority of readers will have little, if any, notion of the *soft* sounds of letters. Too many rules cause confusion. However, rules fulfil short-term objectives. They are expedients.

Success is the only encouragement that someone with reading difficulties needs. Toe by Toe introduces rules which make success inevitable.

People whose lives are not made miserable by reading difficulties use the **soft 'c'** rule unconsciously each time they read words such as cellar, necessary, nice, rice…etc. With habitual usage our students will do the same.

Coach

Listen to the sound of the letter **c** in the following sentence:

Mice were recently seen eating celery in the cellar. You can see that, every **c** makes the sound we normally associate with the letter **s**.

The rule is: **c** followed by **i**, **e** or **y** says: **'s'**

Ask the student to read the polynons on the opposite page. When a polynon has been read correctly, you must tick the first box. Dates and dots are not required. The other box can be ticked when the polynon has been read correctly on another occasion.

If your student has difficulty, ask him/her to read the polynon, syllable by syllable, using the skills developed in the syllable division exercises. The polynons must be divided mentally (no pencils).

Note: This is essentially a reading exercise and ticks are given for <u>reading</u> a polynon and not for dividing it.

Read		
doachace		
fuppancip		
ancippode		
telletrace		
effrancer		
prackpoll		
ickarrick		
itchercell		
cellitadgee		
cipkiss		
apcishon		
crandice		
cinnolts		

Read		
naimonice		
loncerich		
cistellite		
cimmelt		
epcurling		
cillarder		
ettockill		
sunnice		
lapcerrome		
cammdock		
cishtick		
eppodcill		
alcertop		

Read		
minnertice		
isherclint		
cipponnash		
cerdommate		
ancimmid		
illercinnog		
ciskernoad		
ancillend		
trishercans		
dromcitch		
amcernel		
castick		
raddancil		

Read		
cerrebode		
baccomitch		
mancideem		
francidock		
enceripe		
banceemoal		
suncidane		
camilope		
clancerderm		
skanderice		
citcherderp		
libancert		
cedrabcern		

Other Information

Real Words

Coach

Make sure your student knows that these are real words.

Each pair of words needs to earn three consecutive ticks.

Each tick must be earned on a different day.

Tick the positives and dot the negatives.

Make sure you work on any negatives before you leave the page.

		Day										Day							
		Month										Month							
cellar	recite								brace	census								
citizen	civilised								Percy	decimal								
dancer	celebrate								mercy	cinema								
fencing	deceased								trace	place								
fencer	specific								civil	placid								
grace	specify								force	rancid								
traced	pacify								dance	cygnet								
forcing	precedent								cystic	acidity								
cement	decimate								decide	entice								
concern	cinders								cider	acid								
central	circus								recede	concept								
cynical	price								concise	racing								
love	while								always	once								

Other Information

Sentences / Passages

When students reach this stage of the manual we can be confident that their word building skills will be advanced enough to utilise the context in the reading of non-phonic words.

The word 'sense' appears in this exercise. The final 'e' is not pronounced and the rule for **mute 'e'** is not invoked. The student will learn the word through the coach's prompts and the word's relations with other elements of the sentence.

Coach

Ask the student to read the sentences. If all the words are read correctly tick the box.

1. Underline any words in a sentence which have not been read correctly and coach them.

2. After a period of **not less** than twenty-four hours you must ask the student to attempt the underlined words once more. When the student knows the word put a bar (/) through the underline with a pencil.

3. Tick the box when all the underlined words in a sentence have been barred. Dates are not required. However, you must keep returning to the underlined words until all boxes have been ticked.

The full sentence needs to be read once only but the underlined words must then be coached.

Never bar a word on the day that you coach it.

"Lice are the price one has paid for living the life of a vagabond," explained Cecil the celebrated cynic from Manchester. Cyril conceded that Cecil's concern had been noted and from now on he would attempt to lead a more civilised life in a proper home so he went to the clinic   and was at once given the shampoo.

Mice and rats are not very nice. Sometimes they eat cheese and rice. Soap and celery mixed with spice are always eaten with toast. Rats love cardboard. Mice are much more civilised in their habits and are dainty eaters while rats are not in the least concerned with good manners and always leave a dreadful mess. "Love and kisses will not wash the dishes or put bread in the larder," said Fred.

A large black cinder was the only trace left of the once cherished van. "This may take a while," said the leading fireman, shaking his head as he watched the blaze. Forty shovels of sand and one full bag of cement are needed to make enough mortar to erect the central pillar in the cellar under the cinema. "Take my advice and don't eat too much rice because once you reach the other side you may find that rice will be the only food you eat for a while," grinned the traveller.

Other Information

Hard & Soft 'c' combinations

This exercise may seem difficult but students pick up the rules quickly.

Coach

The letters **cc** make distinctly different sounds. Listen to the sound they make in the words **accident** and **accent**. Then listen to the sound they make in the words **occult** and **account**. In the first pair of words, the letters **e** and **i** determine the sound of the letters that precede them. They have the power to change the sound of the second **c** into the sound of the letter **s**. Without the letters **e** or **i** to assert their influence, the double **c** in the second pair of words keeps one hard sound alone.

In the shaded area you will find examples of the syllable division which we use as a warming up exercise for real words. In the first example column of shaded polynons the letters **cc** take the hard and soft sounds and the divide is through the middle: **c/c**. In the second shaded column the polynons are divided as any twin consonants: **cc/**.

Ask the student to make one division only. The pencil stroke should be made **between** or **after** the **twin c** polynons in the unshaded area. When the polynons have been successfully divided, ask your student to *attempt* to read them. Do not be too strict. If the proper sound is given to the double **c** you can consider it read correctly.

Ticks and dots are not needed but good coaching is!

Hard 'c' + Soft 'c'. Hard 'c' only		A mixture of both sounds. Divide with a pencil.
accident	**hiccup**	**Make one division only: c/c or cc/**
ac/celmer	unacc/url	iccipode	succonding
oc/cinaster	pecc/opent	taccellot	niccomrit
ac/cidorm	dacc/omman	accimoat	occimet
oc/cinpome	tecc/oshin	saccolter	macconer
inac/ceptop	mecc/anoat	eccertope	vaccondail
mac/cinack	occ/uldip	inaccind	laccodime
anic/cipone	ecc/anail	lacconder	baccomine
inuc/cibeen	ticc/onder	accitoab	iccelling
ic/cinders	lacc/oppid	laccapram	occitain
inac/certent	sacc/onoaf	accertone	accottain
ec/celeen	hicc/under	eccoanlab	imiccerop
ec/cillaft	unocc/anail	occirgoad	teccampod

Other Information

Real words with 'cc'

Many of the coached words in this exercise will be unfamiliar and difficult. They will prove the effectiveness of the Toe by Toe word-building technique.

In a structured exercise such as this 'difficulty' is not a deterrent. Students like to grapple with the sound and they draw confidence as the **'cc'** begins to operate on the sound of the whole word.

Coach

Some of the words will be unfamiliar and you will need to coach them. Do not give ticks for coached words but please give praise for effort and assure your student that s/he will read the word correctly at the next attempt. Point out that these are difficult words.

Make sure your student knows that these are real words.

Each pair of words needs to earn three consecutive ticks.

Each tick must be earned on a different day.

Tick the positives and dot the negatives.

Make sure you work on any negatives before you leave the page.

	Day											Day									
	Month											Month									
accident	occupant									broccoli	accidental								
accept	accepted									accosted	accessory								
occupy	eccentric									accredit	succulent								
accused	accusal									occurring	vaccinate								
accede	accurate									accusing	accomplish								
accuse	accuser									Occident	desiccate								
success	succeed									occultist	acclaimed								
access	succinct									occultism	succeeding								
accord	accent									occipital	accelerate								
occult	occurred									accost	accelerator								
acclaim	hiccup									tobacco	accolade								
occur	raccoon									accursed	accordingly								

Other Information

Sentences

Many of the words used in these sentences will seem strange and difficult but we are not primarily interested in widening a student's vocabulary. It doesn't matter that students are unlikely to know the meaning of the word 'occipital'. It does matter that students build words.

Praise for reading a word which a student may never have heard - or know the meaning of - is vital.

Coach

Ask the student to read the sentences. If all the words are read correctly tick the box.

1. Underline any words in a sentence which have not been read correctly and coach them.

2. After a period of **not less** than twenty-four hours you must ask the student to attempt the underlined words once more. When the student knows the word put a bar (/) through the underline with a pencil.

3. Tick the box when all the underlined words in a sentence have been barred. Dates are not required. However, you must keep returning to the underlined words until all boxes have been ticked.

The full sentence needs to be read once only but the underlined words must then be coached.

Never bar a word on the day that you coach it.

The accused claimed that it was an accident but the judge and jury did not agree and sentenced the criminal to a long term of imprisonment.

The coroner said that the occipital injury was made on impact. "This was not made evident in your original statement," accused the barrister.

The eccentric professor had to accept that to accelerate in heavy traffic was a grave error and that the accused had succeeded in making a fool of him.

"Did it not occur to you that the doctor's success in treating the injured driver was only the result of his access to a good first aid kit and not the pressure that was forced on the ambulance driver's accelerator pedal?" said the judge.

"Had the accident victim been vaccinated against tetanus within the last six years he would be able to give an accurate and succinct testimony," said the witness. All the seats had occupants but the assize judge gave his assent for some people to stand at the back but it did not occur to him that they would block the exits. Traces of carpet were discovered in the accused man's pockets. They had also accrued in the crevices of the passenger seat as the occupant was sleeping.

Other Information

'tion, sion, cial, tial, cian'

Polynons are not appropriate for this exercise. The only prerequisite for reading real words is the ability to recognise word endings quickly.

Some students may struggle to perfect the pronunciation when they tackle column **A** but the real words will establish this very quickly.

Coach

Listen to the sounds made by the bold letters in the following words:

mention   magician   mission

The sound made by the bold letters is **sh'n -** rather like the word **shun** without the vowel. Once more listen to the sound of the bold letters:

social   initial

This time the bold letters say **sh'l;** which is rather like the word **shall** without the vowel. Establish the sounds by repeating the words.

Ask the student to read the word endings listed in pairs in column **A**. When you are confident that s/he can read them quickly and correctly you may move to the next columns of real words.

If your student has difficulty with a word you can ask them to try both sounds of the vowel. Most difficulties will arise when the student reads a word such as 'lotion' and gives the first **o** its short sound.

Remember: In the word columns both words must be read correctly to earn a tick. Coached words receive a dot.

A				Day									Day							
---	---	---	---	Month	---	---	---	---	---	---	---	---	Month	---	---	---	---	---	---	---
tion	tian	emotion	tactician								mansion	precision								
cian	tion	passion	magician								sanction	invasion								
cial	tial	tension	addition								action	potion								
sion	tion	invention	special								spatial	notion								
tial	cial	detention	politician								division	induction								
cian	sion	mention	initial								function	portion								
cial	tion	vision	incision								motion	ration								
tial	tian	official	partial								lotion	attention								
sion	cial	traction	martial								partition	section								
tion	tial	fraction	caption								potential	station								
cian	tial	suction	option								session	elation								
sion	cial	nation	diction								revision	social								
cial	sion	question	decision								petition	aversion								
tion	tial	essential	facial								pollution	retention								
cial	tion	pension	adoption								inclusion	mission								

Other Information

Sentences

Coach

Ask the student to read the sentences. If all the words are read correctly tick the box.

1. Underline any words in a sentence which have not been read correctly and coach them.

2. After a period of **not less** than twenty-four hours you must ask the student to attempt the underlined words once more. When the student knows the word put a bar **(/)** through the underline with a pencil.

3. Tick the box when all the underlined words in a sentence have been barred. Dates are not required. However, you must keep returning to the underlined words until all boxes have been ticked.

The full sentence needs to be read once only but the underlined words must then be coached.

Never bar a word on the day that you coach it.

Did the officer mention that it was not the intention of the procession to pass the official residence of the city's leading politician?

In addition to the damp conditions in the sleeping section of the train, an invasion of flies and other insects made sleeping very difficult.

The people passed a motion banning sales of a dark lotion which had started the commotion at the extra special meeting of the women's institution.

Did you hear the proposition giving the officer permission to attack the opposition as they left the railway station?

It is not essential to inspect the woman's credentials but it would be wise to make a close inspection of the official letter and see if it matches her identification tag.

The preparation of food in the prison was not an occasion for cheers of elation because the size of the rations were an insult to the inmate population.

The standing ovation was an expression of the deep satisfaction felt by the men from the plantation at such a grand interpretation of the works of their nation.

Other Information

'le' at the end of a word

The sound made by this combination has always caused problems and it is subject to all manner of regional variations.

The coach should allow for regional patterns of speech.

Coach

Listen to the sound of the bold letters in the following words:

Tunn**el**   bramb**le**   kett**le**   hand**le**   med**al**

'**le**', '**el**', and '**al**' at the end of a word make the same sound. Establish the sound in your head and then make sure that the student is able to repeat the sound after you.

When you are confident that the student is aware of the proper sound you may start the exercise.

Both words in a pair must be read correctly to earn a tick.

		Day											Day								
		Month											Month								
kettle	kettles									credible	dental										
mangle	nettles									sensible	trifle										
dabble	goggles									chuckle	stable										
raffle	raffles									steeple	table										
dapple	apples									straddle	noble										
tussle	beetles									throttle	sable										
cackle	eagles									terrible	cradle										
puzzle	rattles									scribble	stifle										
pickle	pickles									mingle	scandal										
sickle	ripples									syllable	bridle										
handle	handles									possible	cable										
medal	medals									funnel	funnels										
revel	revelled									parcel	parcels										
paddle	candles									principle	able										

Other Information

Sentences

Coach

Ask the student to read the sentences. If all the words are read correctly tick the box.

1. Underline any words in a sentence which have not been read correctly and coach them.

2. After a period of **not less** than twenty-four hours you must ask the student to attempt the underlined words once more. When the student knows the word put a bar **(/)** through the underline with a pencil.

3. Tick the box when all the underlined words in a sentence have been barred. Dates are not required. However, you must keep returning to the underlined words until all boxes have been ticked.

The full sentence needs to be read once only but the underlined words must then be coached.

Never bar a word on the day that you coach it.

Put the candle in the neck of the bottle and place it by the bible near the edge of the table before you travel to the hostel.

If a particle of dust settles on an article of dress it is best cleaned off with a little bit of sticky tape or a damp flannel.

The incredible Mr. Bartle startled his wife by putting the heavy family bible above the living room door and letting it drop upon her unsuspecting head.

There was a terrible commotion when Mrs. Bartle was startled. She went into battle with both broom and heavy kettle, striking hard at the man for his lack of wit and understanding.

The boy in the stable was perfectly able to put the bridle and the saddle on the black horse.

Take the cattle to the middle of the pasture and make sure they don't eat the mistletoe that creeps up the trees.

If you are nimble and don't wake the dog in the kennel you can straddle the branches and help pick the apples which dangle over the stream.

Check any previously completed grids for words which have not earned three ticks in a row.

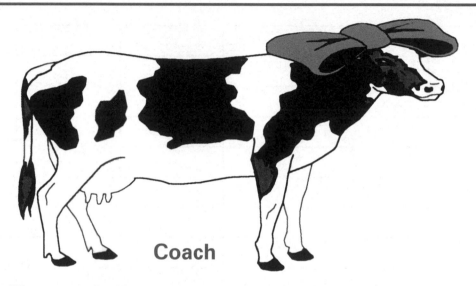

Coach

The letters **ow** make two different sounds. Listen to the sound **ow** as in c**ow**. Listen to the sound **ow** as in gr**ow**. We use a memory aid (mnemonic): **The cow wears a bow.**   Ask your student to study the picture. Make sure s/he is familiar with the two sounds before starting the exercise on the opposite page.

Make sure your student knows that these are real words. Each pair of words needs to earn three consecutive ticks. Each tick must be earned on a different day. Tick the positives and dot the negatives. Make sure you work on any negatives before you leave the page.

The more unusual the memory aid, the more effective it will be. Hence the cow wears the bow on its head rather than its neck.

Day	
Month	

Day	
Month	

'ow' as in cow

clown	clowning
flower	howling
trowel	growling
shower	growled
gown	prowler
brown	crowded
fowl	allowed
scowl	powder
crowd	tower
towel	howled
crown	drowning
cold	behind

'ow' as in low

yellow	own
mellow	glow
slowly	owner
grown	snow
snowing	shallow
throw	blown
flow	grow
bowl	barrow
flown	marrow
blow	stowed
slower	showing
can't	buy

Other Information

Sentences

Coach

Ask the student to read the sentences. If all the words are read correctly tick the box.

1. Underline any words in a sentence which have not been read correctly and coach them.

2. After a period of **not less** than twenty-four hours you must ask the student to attempt the underlined words once more. When the student knows the word put a bar (/) through the underline with a pencil.

3. Tick the box when all the underlined words in a sentence have been barred. Dates are not required. However, you must keep returning to the underlined words until all boxes have been ticked.

The full sentence needs to be read once only but the underlined words must then be coached.

Never bar a word on the day that you coach it.

Your student may need reminding that **le**, **al** and **el** at the end of a word make the same sound.

Rowan trees grow in the woods by the banks of a cold stream which bubbles under the low branches of the willow trees and flows under the bridge that straddles the road. The rowdy cowboy from down Mexico way took a shower but forgot to take off his boots. This action did nothing to impress the sheriff who showed him little sympathy. Just below the window, the prowler had left his tracks in the cold December snow. The wind howled, a dog growled, the window was bolted shut and he left in frustration. The clown standing behind the big top frowned at his fellow performers because they had howled at his accidental antics which had nothing to do with his performance. If you can't find the cash to buy a marrow you may grow one but don't tell the big crowd because the news may filter through to the man in the yellow bowler hat. Behind the clock tower, but above the street level, the smoke billowed over the bowling green, through the gardens and down the twisted streets. The water was shallow and flowed quickly through the meadowlands and on to the forest lakes, which lapped at the slopes of the verdant hills. "You can't do that!", the scowling farmer with the trowel howled at the brown cow.

Other Information

Real words using the 'ou' digraph.

'ou' has many sounds. The 'ou' in the following words: **group, enough, cough,** carries a different sound in each case. This choice of sounds makes polynons inappropriate.

We have listed words with the most common sound.

Coach

Ou can say many things but it usually says **ou** as in **ou**t. Listen to the sound made by the following words:

round   tr**ou**t   l**ou**d

Familiarise yourself with the sound. Make sure the student can repeat the sound before you start the exercise.

Make sure your student knows that these are real words.

Each pair of words needs to earn three consecutive ticks.

Each tick must be earned on a different day.

Tick the positives and dot the negatives.

Make sure you work on any negatives before you leave the page.

	Day		Day
	Month		Month
trout	bound	countess	accountant
round	lout	trounced	announced
about	sour	foundry	impounded
found	clout	abound	confounded
sound	south	spout	foundations
hour	grout	shouted	compounds
mouse	outer	flour	unfounded
pout	arouse	mound	flounder
flout	lounge	louder	roundabout
louse	amount	pouch	groundless
ounce	outing	mouth	boundary
bounce	hound	snout	scoundrel

Other Information

Sentences

The hound bounded through the grounds of the castle until it found and roused the grouse that were living close to the house by the south gate.

The County Housing Department was much too slow to show the new inspector around the accommodation which was too cold for the old man and his wife.

A special train was sent to Southampton to pick up the ground workers who were urgently needed to work on the underground water tunnels.

The cold water fountain will not flow because the water has slowed to a trickle through the network of old and rusty pipes which thread through the cellar.

"As the king was crowned there was heard the astounding sound of the normally loyal royal bandsmen playing some other nation's anthem," Sally explained.

"The accountant's accounts don't show how the pounds were counted out to the woman selling flounders in the market place in Louth," said the tax inspector.

I can vouch that mound upon mound of old pound notes can be found in the dark underground tunnels in the south of the town if you are able to crouch and dig.

Other Information

Polynons using the 'oi' digraph

The student should be familiar with the sound made by the letters **'oy'**.

Mixing both combinations **'oi'** and **'oy'** makes it easier to reinforce the exercise.

Coach

Listen to the sound made by the bold letters in the following words:

co**in**   **f**o**il**   **r**oy**al**   **b**oy   **s**o**il**

Note: 'oi' says 'oy'.

The student is already familiar with the sound made by the letters **oy**. The letters **oi** make the same sound.

This is a reading exercise. The student must observe all the skills. If your student has difficulty, ask him/her to read the polynon, syllable by syllable, using the skills developed in the syllable division exercises. The polynons must be divided mentally (no pencils).

Note: This is essentially a reading exercise and ticks are given for reading a polynon and not for dividing it.

S/he must read the whole polynon before you award a tick.

Each polynon needs to earn three consecutive ticks.

Each tick must be earned on a different day.

Tick the positives and dot the negatives.

Make sure you work on any negatives before you leave the page.

	Day									
	Month									
'oi' as in 'boy'										
sopteroin										
toimerroy										
oyfolpoy										
tremgoifer										
troyfop										
coilbill										
cifferoy										
ploinape										
aloinaft										
ockeroid										
voiditch										

	Day									
	Month									
ploysagger										
cloinerafe										
traimsoib										
cistoiling										
donninoil										
oylertoil										
itchoiling										
coymender										
cidderpath										
chenneroid										
boyloid										
parratoin										

Other Information

'oi' & 'oy' - real words

Coach

Coach

Make sure your student knows that these are real words.

Each pair of words needs to earn three consecutive ticks.

Each tick must be earned on a different day.

Tick the positives and dot the negatives.

Make sure you work on any negatives before you leave the page.

	Day											Day									
	Month											Month									
soya	voyage										voice	asteroids									
loyal	point										embroil	deployment									
appoint	foil										deploy	paranoid									
joint	soil										spoiled	cloisters									
spoil	coil										join	loitered									
loyalty	boiled										enjoy	employee									
joiner	moist										uncoil	employers									
loin	foist										noisy	ointment									
avoid	toil										foiled	appointed									
royalty	joyful										pointer	moisten									
Savoy	coiled										coin	loincloth									
ploy	toiled										hoist	enjoyment									

Other Information

The Royal Boil

We explained in the introduction why '**Toe by Toe**' does not play games. However, we expect the student to make and enjoy progress. This passage is light and hopefully amusing but its primary function is to test and consolidate the student's newly acquired word building skills.

Coach

Ask the student to read the sentences. If all the words are read correctly tick the box.

1. Underline any words in a sentence which have not been read correctly and coach them.

2. After a period of **not less** than twenty-four hours you must ask the student to attempt the underlined words once more. When the student knows the word put a bar (/) through the underline with a pencil.

3. Tick the box when all the underlined words in a sentence have been barred. Dates are not required. However, you must keep returning to the underlined words until all boxes have been ticked.

The full sentence needs to be read once only but the underlined words must then be coached.

Never bar a word on the day that you coach it.

"Our king has no ease. His boil must be squeezed," the minister quaked.
"But who shall we appoint?" said a voice from the cloisters. "Not I," said the
joiner who loitered by the toilets. "Do we have a choice?" asked the nurse
from the clinic. "If the lump is on his rump it will test their loyalty," said the
boy from the Savoy who was eating saveloys. "You are getting paranoid.
It's a task we can't avoid," said Roy to the maid who was terribly afraid that
she could be the one to take a lance to the lump on that royal rump. "If you
get the appointment you will need lots of ointment to take away the sting
from that mound on our king. You may use talcum powder but if the king's
shouts get louder, you will not avoid that vat of boiling oil which the king has
reserved to dunk those so absurd as to point a sharp lance at that zit beneath
his pants." "What luck and what joy," said the Greek chap from Troy. "What
has happened?" asked the employee from Athens. "No one need toil on that
angry painful boil. Our king without thinking has sat on a sharp spring. The
point of the coil put a hole on the lump, that very septic bump, and now it is
lanced and our king is at ease and may sit where he decrees.

Other Information

Polynons using the digraphs 'au'/'aw'

Day											
Month											
autimmone											
taulerpoy											
awtaiper											
sawlock											
shauloan											
thackpawn											
itchantaw											
scrawboil											
dawlitch											
crawfitch											
thaumer											

Day											
Month											
loinattaul											
rawbition											
auditack											
hipperlaw											
mawcial											
cauchimp											
praukish											
sawkerfoy											
autioning											
crawper											
thaudoat											

Other Information

Real Words

Coach

Make sure your student knows that these are real words.

Each pair of words needs to earn three consecutive ticks.

Each tick must be earned on a different day.

Tick the positives and dot the negatives.

Make sure you work on any negatives before you leave the page.

	Day														Day									
	Month														Month									
raw	paw											caution	prawn									
saw	flaunt											crawling	lawn									
Paul	trauma											drawn	applaud									
yawn	hawk											straw	cause									
haul	daub											pauper	bauble									
haunt	pause											outlaw	sprawl									
taunt	launch											gauntlet	dawn									
crawl	laundry											saunter	drawing									
maul	clawed											trawler	staunch									
fraud	nautical											saucer	jigsaw									
gaudy	sawdust											sauce	jaunt									
gaunt	haunted											jackdaw	audit									

Other Information

Sentences

Having reached the more complex words and their incumbent skills students must be made aware of the more common typefaces (fonts)

All further sentence exercises will be printed in 'Times New Roman' which is probably the most widely used of the typefaces found in newspapers, periodicals, books,… etc

The most drastic change will be found in the lowercase letter: **g**

Coach

Ask the student to read the sentences. If all the words are read correctly tick the box.

1. Underline any words in a sentence which have not been read correctly and coach them.

2. After a period of **not less** than twenty-four hours you must ask the student to attempt the underlined words once more. When the student knows the word put a bar **(/)** through the underline with a pencil.

3. Tick the box when all the underlined words in a sentence have been barred. Dates are not required. However, you must keep returning to the underlined words until all boxes have been ticked.

The full sentence needs to be read once only but the underlined words must then be coached.

Never bar a word on the day that you coach it.

Undaunted, the taunter hurled insults at the stout groundsman but later he was found badly mauled and forlorn, sprawled and crawling on the lawn.

The boy who hauled the heavy rickshaw went to the laundry to pick up the woman who wore the black shawl and took her home.

Does brawn taste like potted meat and does it stick to people's jaws and why did the small rabbit pause to clean its paws?

Maureen and Maud were not in the least overawed by Paul and Claud but Laura and Paul were annoyed with Robert and Kathleen.

The tiger sprang from its haunches and mauled the animal trainer because she taunted it with a long black stick and a feather duster.

"Measure the distance in nautical miles", said the skipper to the hauler of the trawler nets, "and don't mention the haddock when we return."

People who ride bikes or haul heavy goods on causeways can, and often do, cause nasty accidents to people who ride on skateboards or push prams.

Check any previously completed grids for words which have not earned three ticks in a row.

Other Information

The Digraph 'ew'

The examples used for the subtleties of the **'ew'** sound are the words **'you'** and **'who'**

Coach

Listen to the sounds made by the bold letters in the words below:

new   moon

The difference is very slight. In the first word the bold letters seem to say the word **'you'** and in the second word the bold letters make the sound **'oo'** as in m**oo**n.

The choice of sound is determined both by the letters that precede **ew** and, sometimes, where your student lives. Do not be too strict about the sound produced.

Make sure your student knows that these are real words.

Each pair of words needs to earn three consecutive ticks.

Each tick must be earned on a different day.

Tick the positives and dot the negatives.

Make sure you work on any negatives before you leave the page.

Day		Day	
Month		Month	

'ew' can make the sounds 'you' or 'oo' as in 'moon'

new	skewer	brew	grew	
few	ewer	screw	shrewd	
pewter	Dewsbury	shrew	blew	
spew	dew	Andrew	Lewis	
steward	curfew	chewing	brewing	
Kew	newt	brewery	brewed	
mews	fewer	flew	jewels	
Jewish	stewed	drew	crew	
stew	Stewart	strewn	lewd	
dewdrop	stewing	threw	trews	
Newton	pew	slew	withdrew	

Other Information

Sentences

Coach

Ask the student to read the sentences. If all the words are read correctly tick the box.

1. Underline any words in a sentence which have not been read correctly and coach them.

2. After a period of **not less** than twenty-four hours you must ask the student to attempt the underlined words once more. When the student knows the word put a bar **(/)** through the underline with a pencil.

3. Tick the box when all the underlined words in a sentence have been barred. Dates are not required. However, you must keep returning to the underlined words until all boxes have been ticked.

The full sentence needs to be read once only but the underlined words must then be coached.

Never bar a word on the day that you coach it.

The crew of the trawler drew in their nets and placed the fish in the crates before they reached their destination.

It was late August. The avenue was strewn with leaves and rubbish. The pensioner sat on the old pew near the entrance to the Seaman's Mission.

The crew who flew the plane withdrew to the restroom while the others grew tired of waiting for the Station Commander to give them their new orders.

Andrew went to Lewisham before he went to Newmarket but not before Angela Lewis had returned to her new address in a wealthy suburb on the outskirts of Crewe.

She forgot to mention that she had been held in detention because she threw the new girl down the muddy slope at the bottom of the playground.

The heron skewered the fish and then chewed and devoured it before it turned its hungry attention to the newts and toads.

On special occasions he drew his cash from the bank and threw a party for all the new members of the delegation from Dewsbury.

Other Information

The sound of the letter 'a' when it follows 'w'

	Day												Day										
	Month												Month										

Remember! Listen to the sound made by the letters 'wa' in the word wasp.

wash	Walter								swarm	wanton							
ward	swan								swat	wander							
warm	swallow								waddle	want							
wasp	wallow								watch	was							
wart	wad								Watford	Wanda							
war	wadding								Wapping	wallop							
wan	warbler								Swansea	swamp							
wand	reward								warning	warder							
warp	swarthy								warren	waffle							
warn	dwarf								thwart	wallet							
fall	forward								straight	eight							

Other Information

Sentences

Coach

Ask the student to read the sentences. If all the words are read correctly tick the box.

1. Underline any words in a sentence which have not been read correctly and coach them.

2. After a period of **not less** than twenty-four hours you must ask the student to attempt the underlined words once more. When the student knows the word put a bar (/) through the underline with a pencil.

3. Tick the box when all the underlined words in a sentence have been barred. Dates are not required. However, you must keep returning to the underlined words until all boxes have been ticked.

The full sentence needs to be read once only but the underlined words must then be coached.

Never bar a word on the day that you coach it.

Your student may have difficulty with the place names but they are not beyond her/his word building skills.

Walter lost his wallet in Washington and Wanda was warned not to wander but to walk straight forward to the station in Watford.

The bees swarmed above the flower beds and the wasps buzzed around the piles of old litter which were strewn about the grounds of the house.

If you fall and can't walk, take a taxi to the railway station at Watford and get on the train bound for Warrington unless the train for Wapping has arrived on platform eight.

If the train for Wapping arrives on time you may take the next train on the underground to Heathrow and fly from there straight to Washington.

Walter Walton from Watford warmed his hands by the fire while other people washed themselves in water from the clear stream.

" The passengers bound for Warrington will have to swap trains at the next station and take the forward train to Manchester," shouted the man on platform eight.

The prospect of washing all the dirty clothes was too much for the weary woman so she threw them straight into the dustbin and made some tea.

"You can't buy cold food here," said the woman standing behind the shop counter, "I sell hot pies and peas to warm the wandering people on cold days."

Other Information

'qu' 'qua' 'squ' & 'squa'

This exercise deals with four skills but they are so closely related that students experience little difficulty dealing with them.

Coach

The table may look complicated but it is quite easy to follow. Let the bold print be your guide. Your student should know that the letters **qu** say **kw** as in **qu**ick. Make sure s/he does!

Make sure your student knows that these are real words.

Each pair of words needs to earn three consecutive ticks.

Each tick must be earned on a different day.

Tick the positives and dot the negatives.

Make sure you work on any negatives before you leave the page.

Day								
Month								

Day								
Month								

'qu' says 'kw'

queen	quid
quit	liquid
quiz	quell
quill	inquest
quench	quip

'a' after 'qu' says 'o' as in quad

quad	quarterly
quality	quantity
qualify	quash
equality	qualified
quart	quarrel
quarter	quarry

'squ' says 'skw' as in squid

squid	squirt
squint	squeeze
squirm	squeal
squirrel	squinted
squire	squeak

Note the sound of 'squa' as in squad

squat	squash
squad	squabble
squalid	squawk
squats	squads
squaw	squatter
squalor	squaws

Other Information

Sentences

Students often have difficulty with the sound of '**qu**'. These short quirky sentences make students aware of the extensive use of the sound of '**qu**' and help to establish, and make fluent, their ability to read it.

Coach

Ask the student to read the sentences. If all the words are read correctly tick the box.

1. Underline any words in a sentence which have not been read correctly and coach them.

2. After a period of **not less** than twenty-four hours you must ask the student to attempt the underlined words once more. When the student knows the word put a bar **(/)** through the underline with a pencil.

3. Tick the box when all the underlined words in a sentence have been barred. Dates are not required. However, you must keep returning to the underlined words until all boxes have been ticked.

The full sentence needs to be read once only but the underlined words must then be coached.

Never bar a word on the day that you coach it.

A quintet is required to play quickly so don't squeal if I put the liquid on the equipment.

I require a quiver full of arrows and request that you tell me about the quins.

The squadron needs equipment so quit your job in Quebec and return to Queensland.

The quirky quintet will quarrel with you if you squint at the delinquent squirrel in the square.

Quenton ran frequently across the quadrangle to quench his thirst with orange squash.

Did the quads request feather quilts and wear special glasses to correct their squint?

At the Queen's request the quarreling Quaker was served the quail's eggs and squid.

Beat the carpet with a tennis racquet and remove the blocks if the brakes squeal.

A quantity of quavers was ignored by the quartet but not by the conductor who was very upset.

The poor squatter's banquet boasted such treats as cold toast, tepid soup, and stale cakes.

The televised pictures of the operation made the Marquis feel quite squeamish.

The dentist scraped the plaque from the girl's teeth and requested that she rinse her mouth.

Quit your frequent quarreling and quote the number on the 'equipment request' forms.

Squeeze the tube, squander the cash, quit smoking, quote the rule book and inquire politely.

Other Information

Sentences/Passages Using a Mixture of Skills

As the student's skills increase short passages become more appropriate and certainly less boring. The content of certain passages may be a little exotic for many students. However, we need the student to build words and a predictable context means that educated guesses become a substitute for word building.

Coach

Ask the student to read the sentences/passages. If all the words are read correctly tick the box.

1. Underline any words in a sentence which have not been read correctly and coach them.

2. After a period of **not less** than twenty-four hours you must ask the student to attempt the underlined words once more. When the student knows the word put a bar (/) through the underline with a pencil.

3. Tick the box when all the underlined words in a sentence have been barred. Dates are not required. You must keep returning to the underlined words until all boxes have been ticked.

The full sentence needs to be read once only but the underlined words must then be coached.

Never bar a word on the day that you coach it.

"Can you qualify those remarks or not," interrupted the old judge but the defendant was not to be put off: "I think it is more than likely that you were asleep as my counsel was speaking for me, so , in reply to your question: Yes, I can qualify my remarks but I will not," returned the defendant. "What! What! I have never been so insulted," bawled the Queen's Counsel angrily.

"If you can't hear my case without falling asleep then I suggest that it is for you to quit or at least have the manners not to snore quite so loudly as you squander the taxpayer's cash." There was a low muttering sound from the direction of the bench. The judge looked with horror at the defendant and then at the floor. He began to speak but before he could utter a word he turned quite red. He lifted his gavel and threw it across the room; striking one of the female ushers on the temple. The poor woman let out a scream and then fell stone dead to the floor. The fearful gallery rose in astonishment. The old judge's anger quickly turned to cold fear and then terror. He gripped his chest, lurched forward and expired to the applause of the defendant who was overawed by the accuracy and distance of the late judge's throw.

Other Information

The Letters '*ies*' at the End of a Word

Coach

ies at the end of a word can say **'izz'** as in fi**zz** or **'ize'** as in pr**ize**.

Familiarise your student with these sounds.

You may need to remind the student of the choice of sounds. Ask him/her to think of the word before it is spoken aloud. Once this is done the first answer counts.
Students usually make mistakes with the first few words but their skills develop by the time they reach the second column.

Make sure your student knows that these are real words.

Each pair of words needs to earn three consecutive ticks.

Each tick must be earned on a different day.

Tick the positives and dot the negatives.

Make sure you work on any negatives before you leave the page.

	Day									Day							
	Month									Month							

'ies' can say 'izz' as in fizz *or* 'ies' can say 'ize' as in prize

ferries	hankies		complies	activities	
carries	berries		horrifies	factories	
marries	lorries		liveries	centuries	
nappies	cherries		faculties	deliveries	
applies	replies		dowries	embassies	
supplies	denies		fallacies	difficulties	
dries	fancies		policies	qualities	
fries	tries		remedies	quantities	
cries	lies		arteries	sanctifies	
spies	parties		cities	anchovies	
candies	counties		sundries	territories	

Other Information

Sentences / Passages

Coach

Ask the student to read the sentences / passages. If all the words are read correctly tick the box.

1. Underline any words in a sentence which have not been read correctly and coach them.

2. After a period of **not less** than twenty-four hours you must ask the student to attempt the underlined words once more. When the student knows the word put a bar (/) through the underline with a pencil.

3. Tick the box when all the underlined words in a sentence have been barred. Dates are not required. However, you must keep returning to the underlined words until all boxes have been ticked.

The full sentence needs to be read once only but the underlined words must then be coached.

Never bar a word on the day that you coach it.

Walter could be found in the kitchen garden where he grew blackberries, strawberries, gooseberries and many different types of vegetables such as brussels sprouts, parsnips, leeks and marrows. The different companies were all represented at the exhibition but some had bigger and better trade stands than others and they enjoyed good access to supplies of refreshments and general information. The smaller firms were unhappy because officials had not sent replies to their many complaints. "The rules apply to everyone," said the manager. "But who complies with the rules?" the old man complained bitterly to a steward who was taking advantage of the free food and drink which had been lavished on people from some of the larger companies. "All the stories about the activities of the ladies tug of war team vary from person to person," explained the referee from Blackburn.

"They are no different in context from those we often hear concerning the men's team," returned the Vice Captain who much preferred her team to be called the 'Women's Pull for Peace but Take no Prisoners on a Down Advantage or a Muddy Pitch Wanderers'. Many of the women did not cherish this attempt to extend their title because it would turn the completion of entry forms into an ordeal by pen and paper. "What worries me," declared a voice from the back in squeaky moral tones, "is the effect on family values." The voice was quickly silenced by flurries of rubbish which fell like snow around her. It was hurled from the galleries above by women who disliked her sympathies.

Other Information

...'ied' at the end of a word

Coach

ied at the end of a word can say '**ide**' as in fr**ied** or '**id**' as in carr**ied**

Familiarise your student with these sounds.

You may need to remind the student of the choice of sounds. Ask him/her to think of the word before it is spoken aloud. Once this is done, the first answer counts. Students usually make mistakes with the first few words but their skills develop by the time they reach the second column.

Make sure your student knows that these are real words.

Each pair of words needs to earn three consecutive ticks.

Each tick must be earned on a different day.

Tick the positives and dot the negatives.

Make sure you work on any negatives before you leave the page.

	Day			Day	
	Month			Month	

'ied' can say 'id' or 'ide'. Note the words *fried* and *worried*

petrified	fried		ferried	complied
hurried	worried		verified	unmarried
supplied	dried		carried	unsatisfied
cried	denied		curried	magnified
replied	studied		terrified	dignified
vilified	fancied		glorified	solidified
defied	spied		clarified	simplified
tried	bullied		mystified	horrified
married	rectified		frenzied	unhurried
stupefied	buried		calcified	quantified
applied	satisfied		salaried	qualified

Other Information

Sentences / Passages

Coach

Ask the student to read the sentences / passages. If all the words are read correctly tick the box.

1. Underline any words in a sentence which have not been read correctly and coach them.

2. After a period of **not less** than twenty-four hours you must ask the student to attempt the underlined words once more. When the student knows the word put a bar (/) through the underline with a pencil.

3. Tick the box when all the underlined words in a sentence have been barred. Dates are not required. However, you must keep returning to the underlined words until all boxes have been ticked.

The full sentence needs to be read once only but the underlined words must then be coached.

Never bar a word on the day that you coach it.

The party was well supplied with a mixture of dried food. Many people applied oil to their exposed faces for protection from the freezing wind. Someone asked if the leader was qualified but no one replied to the question. Accompanied by flurries of snow, the party scurried down the slopes in the hope of reaching shelter before the low sun dropped behind the white peaks of the distant hills.

"Don't run! You will squander your reserves of energy," shouted the leader to those in the front of the squad. Many people were horrified by the sudden increase in the depth of snow. Alarm rose to panic and those at the front of the party hurried away from the rest. Those at the rear became increasingly worried that contact would be lost. The leader was less than helpful. Fearing that he would be exposed as a fraud, he tried in vain to reason with the front party but they defied all his pleas.

They were last seen heading for the bleak escarpment from which there would be no return. Petrified with fear, the party made a last frenzied attempt to reach the shelter, when the sound of helicopter blades hacking the frozen air swelled their ears and hearts with joy.

Other Information

Silent Letters 'w' & 'h'

Coach

The letters **w** and **h** are silent in many English words.

The grid opposite has been divided into two sections. The first column contains word with a **silent w**. Ask your student to ignore the **w** and read the word as normal.

The second column contains words with a **silent h**. Ask your student to ignore the **h** and read the word.

Make sure your student knows that these are real words.

Each pair of words needs to earn three consecutive ticks.

Each tick must be earned on a different day.

Tick the positives and dot the negatives.

Make sure you work on any negatives before you leave the page.

	Day							
	Month							

	Day							
	Month							

Silent 'w'

wrap	wrestle
writ	wrench
wrapper	wreath
wrapping	wrote
written	wrist
wren	wrong
write	wriggle
Norwich	answer
Berwick	wretch
Harwich	wrinkle
wrestler	wrangler
wreck	sword
though	great

Silent 'h'

while	whale
whist	whack
white	whim
whiff	whimper
which	ghastly
whether	aghast
whistle	rhubarb
when	gherkin
whelk	ghetto
wheeze	honest
wheel	rhythm
wheat	whipped
straight	break

Other Information

Sentences / Passages

Coach

Ask the student to read the sentences / passages. If all the words are read correctly tick the box.

1. Underline any words in a sentence which have not been read correctly and coach them.

2. After a period of **not less** than twenty-four hours you must ask the student to attempt the underlined words once more. When the student knows the word put a bar (/) through the underline with a pencil.

3. Tick the box when all the underlined words in a sentence have been barred. Dates are not required. However, you must keep returning to the underlined words until all boxes have been ticked.

The full sentence needs to be read once only but the underlined words must then be coached.

Never bar a word on the day that you coach it.

The white bear stood on the packed ice. Raising a terrifying paw the animal licked a deep cut. Behind a snowdrift the hunters waited, occasionally wringing their fingers for warmth. The wretched bear, weakened by hunger, shuffled slowly to the edge of the ice. Although the bear was badly hurt and her senses were dulled by pain the hunters knew that this animal would not be an easy kill. That great white bear was not their usual quarry. Fish, seals or geese, when they arrived, were normal game for these men. But they too were driven by hunger. The geese had not arrived and the spring thaw was long overdue. While they were hunting the cries of their hungry children haunted their ears, driving them to take a chance with the hapless animal which had strayed too close to their camp. If the animal were to plunge straight into the water it would wreck their chance of a kill. The men sprang from behind the drift and hurled their spears straight into the bear's flank. A long harpoon was driven deep into the bear's neck. The animal winced and uttered a low growl as she wheeled round to confront her attackers. A terrible paw struck at the air. A break suddenly appeared in the drifting ice on which the men and the great bear confronted each other. Both parties, hunters and quarry, would be divided by a long, straight channel; a break-ice river which, though narrow, would be deadly to cross.

Other Information

The letters 'igh'

Coach

Words which contain the letters **igh** can be read easily if your student follows this simple rule:

Give the **i** its long sound and ignore the **gh**.

Make sure your student knows that these are real words.

Each pair of words needs to earn three consecutive ticks.

Each tick must be earned on a different day.

Tick the positives and dot the negatives.

Make sure you work on any negatives before you leave the page.

	Day											Day									
	Month											Month									

Remember! Give the 'i' its long sound and ignore the 'gh'

sight	sighted											frighten	enlighten									
high	highest											blighted	midnight									
sigh	slight											brighten	sightless									
night	fright											lighten	lighting									
right	light											Brighton	lightning									
tight	might											plight	Wright									
affright	delight											airtight	tightrope									
fight	lighter											nightly	flight									
bright	blight											mighty	alight									
tighten	lightest											higher	tighter									
lightly	fighter											sighed	highway									

Other Information

Sentences / Passages

Coach

Ask the student to read the sentences / passages. If all the words are read correctly tick the box.

1. Underline any words in a sentence which have not been read correctly and coach them.

2. After a period of **not less** than twenty-four hours you must ask the student to attempt the underlined words once more. When the student knows the word put a bar (/) through the underline with a pencil.

3. Tick the box when all the underlined words in a sentence have been barred. Dates are not required. However, you must keep returning to the underlined words until all boxes have been ticked.

The full sentence needs to be read once only but the underlined words must then be coached.

Never bar a word on the day that you coach it.

The hunters were closing in for the kill but mother had other worries. "Take that clean white sheet off Uncle Dave. It's high time you were all in bed," said Mum coldly to the kids whose freezing breath was the only sign that life existed above their snowbound Wellington boots. "Can we hunt him a little bit longer?" asked Nicola who was hiding behind the garden seat. "I am quite cold now," said Uncle Dave whose once curly hair hung lank and straight about his face as a result of the barrage of accurately thrown snowballs. "But you will get warm when we cook you on the fire," added Annie, whose logic was always enlightening. "Terrific Annie, just what I need right now," groaned Uncle Dave. His plight was plain to see; he had a sheet wound tightly round him, restricting his ability to avoid the snowballs with which the infant hunters were pelting him. Andrew had the bright notion that Uncle Dave could be a large bear which had come to maraud their garden. The fresh snow piled high around the pond made it all seem so realistic. Annie had decided that cooked bear might not be quite so palatable when she thought of her own teddy bear. "I think I want to be Florence Nightingale then I could mend his poorly paw," said Annie. "Florence who?" asked Andrew.

Other Information

The letters 'ph'

Words of Greek origin use the letters **'ph'** where we would normally use **'f'**. However, the words themselves are usually phonetic and, once the switch from **'ph'** to **'f'** has been made the student should have little difficulty in reading them.

Coach

Your student may think that these words are difficult to read but once again there is a simple rule:

The rule is that **ph** says **f** as in **ph**one. Ask your student to say the letter **f** when s/he sees the letters **ph**

Make sure the student can repeat the sound before you start the exercise.

Make sure your student knows that these are real words.

Each pair of words needs to earn three consecutive ticks.

Each tick must be earned on a different day.

Tick the positives and dot the negatives.

Make sure you work on any negatives before you leave the page.

Note! Do not confuse the inability to pronounce a word with a lack of reading skills. Many good readers have difficulty with words such as **phenomenon**

	Day								Day					
	Month								Month					

Remember! 'y' in the middle of a word can take the long or short sound of the letter 'i'

phone	ophthalmic	prophecy	philanthropist
Phyllis	sophistry	prophet	philanthropy
Philip	telephonist	dolphin	alphabet
philosophy	ephemeral	phonetic	phosphorus
phantom	photograph	phlox	telephone
Ralph	emphasis	camphor	emphasize
pheasant	physicist	phonic	pharmacy
phrase	typhoid	physics	pharmacist
phase	typhoon	physical	phlegmatic
autograph	graphic	graphite	phosphate
emphatic	telegraph	nephew	symphony
orphan	sulphur	elephant	cellophane
hyphen	hyphenate	nymph	lymphatic

Other Information

Sentences / Passages

Coach

Ask the student to read the sentences / passages. If all the words are read correctly tick the box.

1. Underline any words in a sentence which have not been read correctly and coach them.

2. After a period of **not less** than twenty-four hours you must ask the student to attempt the underlined words once more. When the student knows the word put a bar **(/)** through the underline with a pencil.

3. Tick the box when all the underlined words in a sentence have been barred. Dates are not required. However, you must keep returning to the underlined words until all boxes have been ticked.

The full sentence needs to be read once only but the underlined words must then be coached.

Never bar a word on the day that you coach it.

A philanthropist gave the misanthrope some food but the misanthrope hated everybody and gave the food to the dogs while the hungry orphans looked on. The philanthropist became very angry and thumped the misanthrope on his nose. He took the orphans to see his friend Ralph, the philosopher, who wore a shabby jacket and odd socks.

Ralph's real name was Randolph and he spoke for some time about a wise old Greek chap called Aristotle. The orphans didn't understand a word and complained bitterly about the smell of sulphur which came from the nearby compost heap.

A telephone engineer worked at the top of the tall telegraph pole at the end of the road. Philip and Phyllis were fond of phoning each other after lunch and if the line was not clear by five o'clock Phyllis would be unable to ask Philip to meet Ralph and Philippa at the Adelphi Playhouse.

Elephants live on the land. Dolphins live in the sea. Phlox are flowers that bloom in August while pheasants hide in the trees. Cellophane wrappers make a mess in the park and pharmacists give pills for disease and like them or not, that Philistine lot, eat telegraph poles for their tea.

Other Information

The letters 'ive' at the end of a word.

The vowel '**i**' in the suffix '**ive**' usually takes the short sound but there are many exceptions to this rule.

Coach

When the letters **ive** occur at the end of a word the vowel '**i**' usually takes the short sound as in the word g**ive**.

Familiarise your student with the sound of the **ive** ending and then ask him/her to read the words in the columns.

Make sure your student knows that these are real words.

Each pair of words needs to earn three consecutive ticks.

Each tick must be earned on a different day.

Tick the positives and dot the negatives.

Make sure you work on any negatives before you leave the page.

		Day											
		Month											
gives	alternatives												
forgive	suggestive												
pensive	explosives												
furtive	constructive												
objective	impressive												
missive	preventative												
massive	corrective												
sensitive	respective												
attractive	aggressive												
olives	unaggressive												
formative	destructive												

		Day											
		Month											
active	incentives												
collective	informative												
restive	instructive												
addictive	affirmative												
tentative	expensive												
positive	attentive												
negative	subversive												
passive	submissive												
selective	reflective												
relatives	decorative												
assertive	imaginative												

Other Information

Sentences

Coach

Ask the student to read the sentences. If all the words are read correctly tick the box.

1. Underline any words in a sentence which have not been read correctly and coach them.

2. After a period of **not less** than twenty-four hours you must ask the student to attempt the underlined words once more. When the student knows the word put a bar **(/)** through the underline with a pencil.

3. Tick the box when all the underlined words in a sentence have been barred. Dates are not required. However, you must keep returning to the underlined words until all boxes have been ticked.

The full sentence needs to be read once only but the underlined words must then be coached.

Never bar a word on the day that you coach it.

There was little alternative but to eat the massive mound of olives.

The woman was said to be both attractive and sensitive.

The author wrote many missives in his formative years.

The treatment was said to be both preventative and corrective.

The large amount of explosives blew a massive hole in the quarry.

The book was informative, imaginative and not too expensive.

It was a collective decision that could not be forgiven.

One man was sensitive while his brother was passive.

The children were always active, often aggressive and very disruptive.

The battery had both positive and negative terminals.

The dog was destructive and never submissive.

A sudden revelation gave him a whole new perspective.

The prospective candidate was dismissive of the opposition.

Formic acid is corrosive and destructive.

Other Information

...xious   ...cious   ...tious   &   ...ous

Coach

The exercise has been divided into two sections. In the first column the words end in the letters **ous**. Ask your student to listen to the sound made by the bold letters in the following words:

marvell**ous**   vigor**ous**

When your student is familiar with the required sound, ask him/her to read the words in the first column. The second column contains words which end in the letters: **cious**, **tious** and **xious**.
All three combinations make the same sound.
Listen to the sound made by the bold letters in the following words:

vi**cious**   an**xious**   cau**tious**

Each pair of words needs to earn three consecutive ticks.

Each tick must be earned on a different day.

Tick the positives and dot the negatives.

Make sure you work on any negatives before you leave the page.

Day								Day							
Month								Month							

Listen to the sound of 'ous' in marvellous and 'cious' in vicious.
Remember!   cious, xious and tious make the same sound.

marvel	marvellous								precious	auspicious							
wonder	wondrous								cautious	suspicious							
ponder	ponderous								vicious	pretentious							
outrage	outrageous								anxious	conscious							
callous	tremendous								noxious	obnoxious							
rigorous	timorous								gracious	fallacious							
joyous	glamorous								delicious	vivacious							
envious	vigorous								spacious	audacious							
porous	scandalous								luscious	bumptious							

Other Information

Sentences

Coach

Ask the student to read the sentences. If all the words are read correctly tick the box.

1. Underline any words in a sentence which have not been read correctly and coach them.

2. After a period of **not less** than twenty-four hours you must ask the student to attempt the underlined words once more. When the student knows the word put a bar **(/)** through the underline with a pencil.

3. Tick the box when all the underlined words in a sentence have been barred. Dates are not required. However, you must keep returning to the underlined words until all boxes have been ticked.

The full sentence needs to be read once only but the underlined words must then be coached.

Never bar a word on the day that you coach it.

If you are anxious you feel distressed and uneasy about something.

If something is noxious it is unpleasant and harmful.

To be gracious is to be pleasing, agreeable and sometimes benevolent.

A room that is spacious is large with lots of space.

If something is delicious it tastes good and is very enjoyable.

People who are obnoxious are rude, offensive, unpleasant and objectionable.

A vivacious person is happy and lively.

To be audacious is to be fearless and clever or impudent and shameless.

If something is precious it is worth a great deal of money.

People who are vicious are hurtful, mean, spiteful and wicked.

A pretentious person thinks they are more important than they are.

A fallacious person can easily mislead you.

A cautious person will never walk under a ladder or skate on thin ice.

Envious people dislike others for their good fortune and success.

Other Information

More Silent Letters

Silent letters are always a problem for students. The words 'christen', 'listen', 'fasten',... etc contain a silent 't'. Students, having reached this exercise, will have sufficient skills to grasp words such as these from the context.

Coach

Once again, some of the words may seem difficult but once your student is aware of the simple rules s/he will find it very easy.

The instructions are written as sub-headings above the exercise.

Make sure your student knows that these are real words.

Each pair of words needs to earn three consecutive ticks.

Each tick must be earned on a different day.

Tick the positives and dot the negatives.

Make sure you work on any negatives before you leave the page.

Long sound of 'i'
ignore the 'g'

sign	signpost
align	aligned
resign	consign
design	malign

'gue' says the hard
sound of 'g' alone
and 'ue' is silent

league	vague
brogue	vogue
epilogue	analogue
rogue	prologue

ignore the 'k'

knee	knit
knife	knew
know	known
knob	knuckle
knock	kneel
knot	knitting

'ch' can say 'k'

chemist	chronicle
anchor	chrysalis
chorus	Chris
loch	chrome
christen	technical
chronic	scheme

Other Information

Sentences

Coach

Ask the student to read the sentences. If all the words are read correctly tick the box.

1. Underline any words in a sentence which have not been read correctly and coach them.

2. After a period of **not less** than twenty-four hours you must ask the student to attempt the underlined words once more. When the student knows the word put a bar (/) through the underline with a pencil.

3. Tick the box when all the underlined words in a sentence have been barred. Dates are not required. However, you must keep returning to the underlined words until all boxes have been ticked.

The full sentence needs to be read once only but the underlined words must then be coached.

Never bar a word on the day that you coach it.

Will she go to the chemist and fetch me some indigestion tablets?

Those blue capsules you gave me for my stomach ache taste atrocious.

The sound of children's voices echoed around the school playground.

Dorothy Docherty went to night-school where she studied technical drawing.

Some chemicals, when ignited, can cause massive explosions.

Christopher the chiropodist went to see the orchestra every Christmas.

The mechanic and his colleague mended the car in a spacious workshop.

A chasm describes a hole which is deep and wide.

Bill Sykes is an obnoxious and vicious character from a Dickens novel.

Shouts of 'resign' were heard from the gallery.

He spoke with a brogue which made me think he was Irish.

"Signing forms may consign one to a life of misery," said the man with a benign smile.

The sight of the black knight from Knutsford made the rogue's knees knock with fear.

Chemists often place too much emphasis on the phosphate content of fertiliser.

Other Information

Real Words

Coach

Make sure your student knows that these are real words.

Each pair of words needs to earn three consecutive ticks.

Each tick must be earned on a different day.

Tick the positives and dot the negatives.

Make sure you work on any negatives before you leave the page.

| Day | | | | | | | | | | | Day | | | | | | | | | |
| Month | | | | | | | | | | | Month | | | | | | | | | |

Three sounds that the combination of the vowels ie/ei can make:

'ie' as in niece

thieves	believe
shield	reprieve
wield	chief
brief	priest
field	piece

'ei' as in neighbour

weigh	neigh
sleigh	vein
reign	beige
veil	freighter
freight	eight
weight	eighty

'ie' as in happier

hardier	luckier
barrier	flimsier
merrier	worrier
terrier	sillier
premier	creamier
windier	farrier
sleepier	prettier
dirtier	fancier
clumsier	harrier
carrier	steadier
pier	stormier
crustier	jollier

Other Information

Sentences / Passages

Coach

Ask the student to read the sentences / passages. If all the words are read correctly tick the box.

1. Underline any words in a sentence which have not been read correctly and coach them.

2. After a period of **not less** than twenty-four hours you must ask the student to attempt the underlined words once more. When the student knows the word put a bar **(/)** through the underline with a pencil.

3. Tick the box when all the underlined words in a sentence have been barred. Dates are not required. However, you must keep returning to the underlined words until all boxes have been ticked.

The full sentence needs to be read once only but the underlined words must then be coached.

Never bar a word on the day that you coach it.

"I believe the chief of the thieves should get a reprieve," said the priest. "Not during my reign!" snapped the Queen who reigned supreme. The Premier, who was always a worrier and not much of a warrior, agreed and blustered, "Your realm is much steadier with that thief behind bars. The judge should have given him eighty years not eight." "Perhaps eighteen years would have been a better sentence," interrupted Her Royal Highness. "What was his crime?" asked the Official Philosopher Royal. "He came from the cold North where the people are hardier, jollier and friendlier," replied the Premier. "Oh dear! Oh dear!" Sir Randolph, the Home Secretary murmured, "What an enormous crime! One of such magnitude should command a sentence with the full weight of the law behind it."

"Transport him to a far off rugged land where he cannot get into mischief," bawled the Queen in the Chief Prison Officer's ear. The priest, for some relief, took a piece of cake from the tray in the foyer when in came the Chancellor wielding the mace above his head. "Put it down at once!" yelled the Queen in disbelief. The Chancellor was taken by surprise and fumbled an apology. "I was only going to pawn it for a day or two and after all it's not as if you need it. The House of Commons is closed and the 'Lords' are all asleep. The judges can rule the land while we find some relief from the endless daily tensions and stresses of power and take the weight off our feet. We will transport him by freighter. He will arrive a little later, tired, dirtier and crated but it will be cheaper by far than to send him by air. The judges can make the laws while we play outdoors. Dangerous people who are happy in spite of their conditions should be thrown into prison and only when they are contrite may they be allowed to see the light."

Other information

Real Words

These words provide the icing on the **Toe by Toe** cake. When students have tackled these words successfully their self-esteem is almost tangible.

Plenty of support and good coaching during the first attempts will lead to a sense of achievement that only those people with reading difficulties can fully appreciate.

Coach

Your student may be forgiven for thinking that some of these words are not real words. They *are* difficult but your student *will* read them.

The **silent b** section is easy. Your student should ignore the **b** and read the word.

The silent **p** and **eu** section is much easier than it looks. Follow the guides on the grid and give the **o** its long sound.

The second column is even easier. The column begins with the word psycho. The **p** is silent, the **ch** says **'c'** as in chemist. Once your student has established this word, s/he will have learned the first half of all but two words in the entire column. The remaining words have **psych** instead of **psycho**.

In the **silent b** section both words need to be read correctly to earn a tick.

Each tick must be earned on a different day.

Tick the positives and dot the negatives.

Make sure you work on any negatives before you leave the page.

Day

Month

Day

Month

Silent 'b'

plumb	plumber
numb	numbness
debt	indebted
subtle	thumb
comb	bomb
climb	climber

'p' is silent, 'eu' says 'you' or 'oo' as in moon

pseudonym

pseudo

pneumonia

pneumatic

pneumogastric

Silent 'p'

psycho

psychology

psychological

psychic

psychosomatic

Psychoanalysis

psychiatric

psychotic

psychosis

psychopath

psychopathic

psychiatrist

Other Information

Sentences / Passages

Coach

Ask the student to read the sentences / passages. If all the words are read correctly tick the box.

1. Underline any words in a sentence which have not been read correctly and coach them.

2. After a period of **not less** than twenty-four hours you must ask the student to attempt the underlined words once more. When the student knows the word put a bar **(/)** through the underline with a pencil.

3. Tick the box when all the underlined words in a sentence have been barred. Dates are not required. However, you must keep returning to the underlined words until all boxes have been ticked.

The full sentence needs to be read once only but the underlined words must then be coached.

Never bar a word on the day that you coach it.

Christopher stared out of the window and then began to draw an elaborate doodle on the inner cover of his English exercise book. It would soon be time to annoy some of the nearby children; a boy here, a girl there, whiling away his time until the last bell sounded an end to the day's monotony. He had been taking notes from the blackboard but the teacher rubbed out the first part before he could write it down. No matter how hard he tried he could not write fast enough to keep up with the rest.

He had to keep looking back at the blackboard. He looked for the word he had started to write – it began with 'th' but so many of the words began with 'th' – which one was it? Too late! The teacher had rubbed it out and she had begun to write another sentence. The word Christopher had been looking for was somewhere in a white cloud of chalk-dust swirling below the blackboard rubber.

The others scribbled away. Why couldn't he do that? He asked himself this question over and over again. He could play chess better than the others, draw fantastic things, construct skyscrapers from 'Lego' bricks. He was imaginative and clever and when he looked out of the window he could see marvellous things and he had wonderful ideas – at least until the teacher noticed him. School made him unhappy.

I used to be like Christopher. My reports always said things like: could do better, needs to pay attention, lacks concentration, results are disappointing, finds time for conversation but not for comprehension, seems to prefer detention to homework, I think I should mention that your son finds time for relaxation at the expense of his education.

But now I can read words like **chiropodist**, **philatelist**, **emphasis**, and **psychologist** because I have learned to build words by using the smallest steps of all: **Toe by Toe**.

Congratulations to coach and student. You have completed your final exercise.

Toe by Toe
8 Green Road, Baildon,
West Yorkshire
BD17 5HL
England

For new orders and details of school discounts:

Phone: 01274 - 598807
Fax: 01274 - 582630
e-mail: info@toe-by-toe.co.uk

Further information is available on our website at:

www.toe-by-toe.co.uk